DATE DUE	RETURNED
OCT 2 8 2011	OCT 3 1 2011

ACE RECORDS

black dog
publishing
london uk

DAVID STUBBS

FOREWORD

I started listening to AFN Stuttgart when I was about 14. I learned about it from a friend—we used to cycle home from school together and discuss the records that we'd heard on the radio the night before. We didn't have any records of our own then, just the radio, but my friend's older brothers did—records by people like Wynonie 'Mr Blues' Harris, Fats Domino, The Hollywood Flames, Chuck Berry and Bill Haley. We knew all the lyrics, and would cycle from school singing "roll over Beethoven and dig those rhythm and blues". We loved that line. Such irreverence in 1956!

Many people listened to American Forces Network (AFN) and Radio Luxembourg then; you couldn't hear decent records anywhere else, certainly not on the BBC's *Light Programme* or *Home Service*, or on Radio Eireann. AFN had been broadcasting from several transmitters in Germany since 1945. Their purpose was to entertain the American troops stationed in Europe, but the American Government soon became aware that they were attracting a huge 'shadow' audience, reputed at one time to number over 50 million listeners. Young people across Europe—starved of decent pop music by their own European stations—would lap up the nourishing diet of pop, R&B, country and rock'n'roll served up by the station. Most people in England and Ireland listened to AFN Stuttgart, as it broadcast from a powerful 100 Kw transmitter, one of several captured from the Germans at the end of the Second World War. The signal came in loud and clear, especially at night.

I had an old valve radio under my bed which I listened to incessantly. It was supposed to be turned off by 11pm, but it had a loose speaker wire so I would simply disconnect this and could continue listening to a crystal clear, low volume signal that was audible direct from the valves. My staple diet was AFN, Radio Luxembourg and Willis Conover's *Late Night Jazz Hour* on Voice of America.

Most nights I would be lulled to sleep by the dulcet tones of Conover as he carefully listed the names of all of the musicians who had played on the jazz classic he had just finished spinning. Although I loved jazz, I preferred the rock'n'roll and R&B records that the station pumped out on programmes such as *Bouncing in Bavaria*, *The Rockin' Sound* and *R&B Showcase*.

Little did I know that, 20 years later, I would be privileged to help found and work for an organisation—Ace Records—that fulfilled a role similar to these stations in introducing millions of eager fans to the, often obscure, but wonderful sounds of that and later eras.

Ted Carroll—September 2007

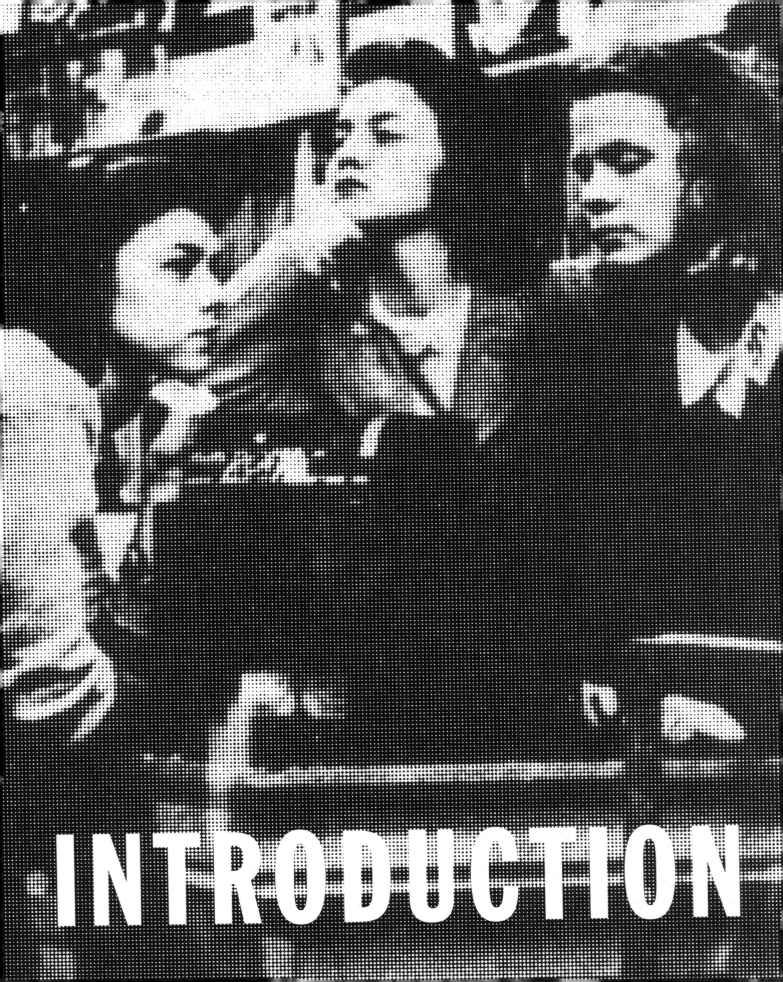

INTRODUCTION

INTRODUCTION

"Although we're dealing in reissues, we're not dealing in nostalgia", insists Roger Armstrong, co-founder of Ace Records (along with Trevor Churchill and Ted Carroll).

It's not nostalgia—because these are recordings many people will be hearing for the first time. It's about fresh discoveries, whether younger people coming to the music fresh, or old hands hearing records sufficiently obscure as to have passed them by first time out. We all have our favourite records from years back but there's nothing as thrilling as hearing an old 45 for the first time and being knocked on your ear by it. For us, you get that same feeling going through the vaults and unearthing a previously unissued recording that just makes you go 'wow!'

Armstrong, Churchill and Carroll first met through their mutual love of records. Then, in the rumbling, pub rock era that preceded punk, they founded a record label, Chiswick Records—bashing onto wax the first recordings by Joe Strummer, Simple Minds' Jim Kerr and the late Kirsty MacColl, and many more. Then, the 1980s arrived and, with the onset of video among other things, they realised that they could no longer compete with large corporate labels for hits; Chiswick was wound down. Ace—and later, its various subsidiary labels—was brought into being (primarily as a reissue label) when Chiswick cut a licensing deal with EMI in 1978. Ace eventually became the mainstay of the company. Given the passion of its three founding directors for the music of the past, this seems inevitable.

To some, Ace might appear to be little more than specialists in the relics of an obscure past, lost in a world where Little Richard remains forever young and The Beatles have yet to emerge. However, there is so much more to the label than that. Not only are they a model of how to run a record company both decently and expertly ("No one can give the quality of service and intelligence of marketing that Ace does with all their products", said legendary American independent label owner, Hy Weiss, in 1995) they have been key players in music history itself. As we will see, they were midwives for early punk and a model for the indie ethos which followed. Had it not been for Chiswick's efforts, artists such as Joe Strummer, Shane MacGowan, Billy Bragg and even Jim Kerr, might have been sufficiently discouraged to jack it all in. Moreover, without Chiswick's example, other small labels might not have sprung up as easily, especially with corporate labels cherry picking the major punk players.

It was Armstrong who, in the 1980s, chaired the meetings that coined the phrase 'world music', and helped artists from Africa, Asia and beyond—who had struggled to find a niche in the Western marketplace; to disseminate their wares more effectively. Rather than merely dwell in the past, Ace looks to restore it anew, through the extensive pool of knowledge of their consultants and archive researchers as well as their admirable, at times foolhardy, physical efforts in rescuing lost acetates and master tapes from garages and warehouses where they might otherwise have been lost for good. Ace also understand the interconnections, the network of bridges between past and present, commerce and soul, rock and R&B, white and black, the superstars and the esoteric. "When I was in my teens I learned about the blues, in part due to my exposure to people like The Yardbirds and The Stones", says Armstrong.

> Through them, I got into Howling Wolf, whom I later realised was Chicago Blues and then into T-Bone Walker—who was the godfather of them all anyway—then Texas blues… it was a point of introduction. And while some people accuse rock artists of ripping off the blues, a lot of these blues guys have said: 'If it wasn't for these rock kids, we wouldn't have made as much money as we did.' Europe has always been the melting pot for American roots music that America isn't.

This process continued with the 1980s garage and rockabilly groups who, by filtering their sounds through punk, created spikier and upgraded versions of rockabilly. Or the acid jazz brigade, nurtured through Ace's Beat Goes Public label, which moved backward to go forward, via rediscovered funk and jazz. As Carroll comments:

> Ace was inspired by such labels as the London label from the 1950s and 60s, and the Sue label from the 1960s. These labels introduced us, and thousands like us across Europe, to the exciting records that were being released in

OPPOSITE:

(Left to right) David Walker (manager of Rocky Sharpe & The Replays), Ted Carroll (Ace Director), Helen Highwater (RS) Trevor Churchill (Ace Director), Martin Barter (EMI), Johnny Stud (RS), Roger Armstrong (Ace Director), Rocky Sharpe & Eric Rondo (RS), circa 1980s.

America on small labels such as Sun, Chess, Atlantic, Imperial, as well as dozens of other more obscure American independents. We came to trust labels such as Sue and London, as we could depend on the fact that almost anything released by them was worth investigating.

We wanted people to be able to depend on Ace in the same way, as a reliable source for great American music from the past, so that when we released an album by say, Johnny Olenn, people would check it out and discover what a great album it was.

"One of the things that gave many of those early recordings their flavour is that they often didn't quite know what they were doing", says Armstrong:

> Often bands would record in radio stations while on the road, or a local entrepreneur might set up a studio in a shack. There's something about those old recordings—it's like the difference between a black and white photo versus a modern colour shot—there's an immediacy about an old black and white image, an atmosphere, a moment captured—no photoshopping.

Those who have been central to Ace since its inception—Churchill, Carroll, Armstrong, Ray Topping, Ady Croasdell, Carol Fawcett—all remember a time when the music they reissue today in such abundance was scarce; a precious resource which a select coterie were obliged to seek out avidly. It was not played by British Radio; stores contained little of it. "You just had to pick up what you could, where you could", says Armstrong:

> You might hear it on American Forces Network or Radio Luxembourg but mostly it was something you would hear from your mates…. You picked it up in a really random way. With jazz, for instance, one of the first things I came across was by Oscar Brown Jr. I loved that record to death, I adored it but I didn't know where it was from, its context or anything.

Ace consultant, Peter Gibbon, meanwhile, recalls going to Frinton beach with his friends and flashing lights at the various pirate radio stations operating offshore. "It was just to let them know we were out there, that they had an

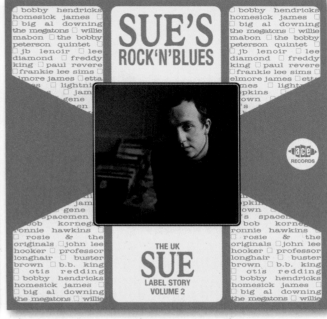

OPPOSITE TOP TO BOTTOM:
Howling Wolf's *Sings The Blues*
(original Crown Records design), 2004,
and Oscar Brown Jr's *Kicks!*, 2004.

ABOVE:
The UK Sue Label Story Vol 1–4, 2004–2006.
Guy Stevens was one of the inspirations for
Ace Records, having (re)issued American
R&B, rock'n'roll and soul records in the
1960s in Britain on his Sue Records label.

audience. People—having been exposed to pretty much whatever music they
want to hear for about 30 years now—forget the sheer paucity of choice that
existed back in the 1950s." It's one of the abiding ironies of Ace's excellent
work—ensuring that future generations don't go through the musical
deprivations they had to endure—that they have assisted in rather spoiling the
present generation, for whom the acquisition of music is perhaps a little too
easy. Today, the problem is where to begin.

Take Ace's own catalogue. Go through it and you will find works by instrumental
group The Ventures, New Orleans pianist Allen Toussaint, Rufus Thomas,
Super Rail Band of the Buffet Hotel de la Gare de Bamako, Mali, Soft Machine,
rock'n'roll twangsters The Rockin' Rebels, Radio Stars, The Players Association,
Phil Ochs, Moon Mullican, Oscar McLollie and His Honey Jumpers, Ellis

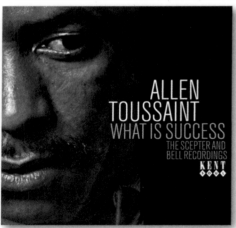

Marsalis (father of Wynton and Branford), Love (their short-lived period with Blue Thumb Records), Alias Ron Kavana, Chuck Jackson, the mouth harp maestro Walter 'Mumbles' Horton, country rock pioneers The Gosdin Brothers, acid rock fanatics Frumious Bandersnatch, The Emotions, Bo Diddley, Steve Cropper, Pop Staples & Albert King (*Jammed Together*), The Charlatans (not the 1990s variety) and The Bugs and Frankie Avalon. Any attempt to define what Ace is 'about', it exceeds. They're not avant-garde, except when they are (John Fahey). They're not about late 1960s prog rock, except when they are (Soft Machine).

Yet despite this abundance, Ace's people are impelled by an abiding love of the rare, the sacrosanct. Tony Rounce, Ace repertoire consultant, speaks candidly when describing the experience of holding the master tape of Hank Ballard & The Midnighters' "Work With Me Annie" in his hand:

> There's a record I've loved pretty much all my life. That's some feeling. And it's something that very few people will ever get to do. I wouldn't quite say it was orgasmic, but it's pretty special. One of the main things that everybody will stress to you about Ace is that nobody here will ever lose their love of music. Even now, we all get excited when we issue something that we've been after for ages.

Certainly, there is a love of the vintage, the authentic, the fixed, the chromium-plated classic about the people who run Ace and those who consume its product—leading grown men to accumulate quite absurdly extensive record collections; more music than they could possibly hope to listen to in a lifetime. Carroll admits—self-deprecatingly—that it is a bit of a "blokey" thing: "Guys like making lists and collecting stuff." However, Vicki Fox, who worked at Rock On with Carroll, respectfully begs to differ. "Women can hoard things just as well as men", she says, "there's more women into it than you would think. But then, Ace always had women working for them, which makes for a better balance, it never felt like an all-bloke's thing."

Despite the apparent equality proffered by Ace, Armstrong admits that its reissue wing caters to a largely white, male audience. There are certainly exceptions to that, as we shall see. However, as the Ace compilation, *Land of 1,000 Dances* illustrates—with its compendium of dance styles including 'the greasy frog', 'the boomerang', 'the dip', 'the sissy', turning over on what must have been a weekly basis—black American music has often been a forward-looking urge, impelled in the 1960s by social circumstance.

Ace doesn't merely fetishise the artists of the past. One of the strongest characteristics of the label is its empathy for the music and musicians. This is coupled with a determination to ensure that their product has the best possible sound, along with thorough background notes and is presented to the best of their abilities. There is devotion and a thoughtfulness that is followed throughout. This means actively seeking out the artists and making sure they get paid properly—which often entails going one step further than even the law requires, especially with regards to copyright.

"We believe it is absolutely essential to pay people; to the extent that we are opposed to the current copyright expiry term", explains Armstrong:

OPPOSITE CLOCKWISE FROM TOP:
The Soft Machine's *The Soft Machine*, 1989; John Fahey's *Fare Forward Voyagers (Soldier's Choice)*, 2007; and Allen Toussaint's *What Is Success*, 2007.

ABOVE LEFT TO RIGHT AND BOTTOM:
Moon Mullican's *Seven Nights to Rock*, 2004; Chuck Jackson's *Good Things*, 1990; Bo Diddley's *Bo's Blues*, 1993; The Charlatans' *The Amazing Charlatans*, 1996; and *Land of 1,000 Dances*, 1999.

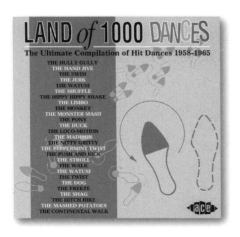

Even if something is out of copyright, we will still pay the artists; we don't try to avoid our responsibilities there.... While people like Bono and Cliff Richard may not need the money, there are people who do—the vast majority of working musicians earn their money in several ways and one of them is royalties. When they reach their 60s or 70s, they're arthritic or can't play any more, they really need that money. You realise people have this misconception about musicians— they divide them up into the losers, the ones who blew it all or got into drugs, or the winners; the big superstars. But the truth is, the big chunk of musicians in the middle, are the ones who just make a regular living out of music but depend on copyright in their recordings as a source of income.

In a music business that is increasingly super-sized, mediocre and plain dirty, Ace are a pearl of an exception—small, immaculate, clean, rare quality. Good rocking, good people, good stories. This is theirs.

ABOVE:
The Ace 'girls': Tracey Hill, Jessica Rant, Yvette De Roy and Nicky McCarthy in the warehouse, circa early 1980s. Image courtesy of Roger Armstrong.

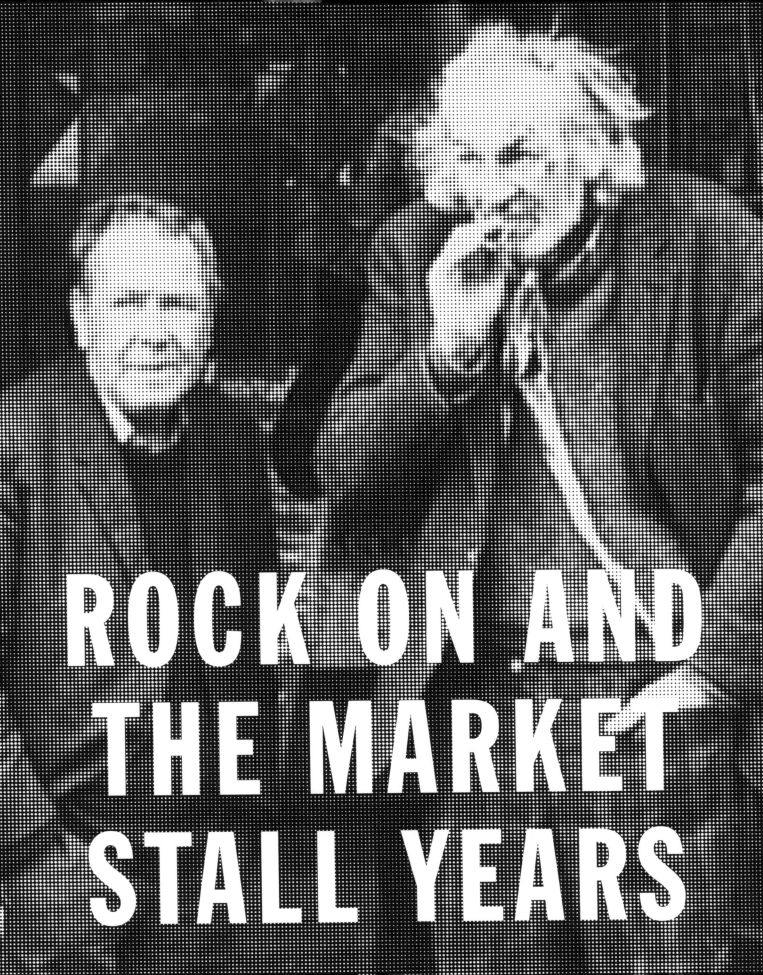

ROCK ON AND
THE MARKET
STALL YEARS

ROCK ON AND THE MARKET STALL YEARS

In the 1960s, there was no Rock On, no Chiswick Records, no Ace. This was what many considered to be rock's halcyon decade, the time in which to enjoy the 'now', a compressed, uninterrupted period of rock history stretching from Beatlemania at one end to Led Zeppelin and Pink Floyd at the other. However, there were a handful of people who felt that vital, if rare and fragile, artefacts of previous and present eras had been overlooked, music such as doo-wop or northern soul which lay beneath the rubble of the 1960s' rock avalanche. "There'd been a double whammy in the 1960s", recalls Charlie Gillett, writer, broadcaster and author of *The Sound of the City* (the first comprehensive attempt to chronicle and document the rise of rock'n'roll):

> First, you had these 'johnny-come-latelys', as I saw them, who thought that nothing had happened before The Beatles and the Rolling Stones. Then, later, the Grateful Dead and people like that came along with their interminable guitar solos. What people who were into this music didn't realise was a) what had gone before and b) what was happening in parallel.

It is not that there was no collectors' scene—since before the Second World War in America, for example, many people would actively seek out and treasure the earliest jazz and blues records. In Britain, jazz fans would hold record recitals in pubs; playing and discussing rare 78s. In the 1960s too, the trade in long-deleted and unavailable doo-wop records had begun to proliferate.

However, while the 1960s party was in full swing, rare indeed were those who felt in any mood for cultural retrospection. Among them, however, was one Rob Finnis, who today works as a consultant on one of Ace's most popular series, *The Golden Age of American Rock'n'Roll*. Travelling across America by Greyhound bus, he tracked down and interviewed many early producers and engineers of the decade—"the backroom boys" as he puts it—including major but temporarily neglected players such as Jerry Wexler and Leiber & Stoller. "It's quite an astonishing thing for him to have done in his teens", says Gillett who, in a brief stint as publisher, commissioned Finnis to write a book about his experiences. (Sadly, it never materialised, although the feel Finnis had for the place and context in which these records were made, was something he introduced into subsequent sleeve notes). "I was very conscious as I wrote *The Sound of the City* that Finnis knew ten times more than I did about the subject matter", admits Gillett. For Gillet, researching *The Sound of the City* in the 1960s was no mean feat:

OPPOSITE TOP TO BOTTOM:

Charlie Gillet DJing in Clapham, circa 1970s, and *Beatlemaniacs!!!*, 2006.

For years, for example, I knew Professor Longhair by name but had absolutely no idea what he sounded like. Things simply weren't available.

Over in America there was a slightly more established scene—the existence of a magazine like *Rolling Stone* meant that if you put out old records, there was a decent chance they'd get reviewed.

Cut back to the early 1960s and Oxford University, where a small coterie of students, including Trevor Churchill and Peter Gibbon (the former, founder/director of Ace Records, the latter a consultant), were ardent fans of such music as doo-wop, early rock'n'roll and 1960s soul. These, they were able to pick up from an unlikely outlet. "There was a very good shop owned by Robert Maxwell", recalls Churchill. "A bookshop, but one that also got literally every new record release in…. So he did one service to humanity there!"

However, Churchill was aware of how the arrival of The Beatles, and the subsequent monomania they engendered, had quashed what—up until that point—had been a diverse and multiple pop culture, in which no particular genre had dominated:

> Beatlemania killed so much of the music people like me loved—many artists who deserved a lot more longevity than they got went to the wall. It certainly killed rock'n'roll—not that it would have survived anyway. Soul only survived because it was so segregated in America back then. 'Thank God', you could almost say from an ironic point of view—because they did survive, this whole slew of crude recordings on shoestring labels.

By the end of the 1960s, however, The Beatles had gone their separate ways. Rock and pop had travelled a long trajectory between 1960 and 1970. Wide-eyed optimism had been cruelly dispelled by events at Altamont while the deaths of Brian Jones, Jimi Hendrix, Jim Morrison and Janis Joplin—all in quick succession—were tragic reminders of the heavy toll taken upon an increasingly heavy music scene.

By 1971, then, there was a hiatus; a sense that a tumultuous chapter had come to a close and a general uncertainty about where things were going next, prevailed. It was in this cultural moment that an increasing number of music fans felt inclined to return to such genres that had been subsumed by the burgeoning rock scene. 1971 was also the year that Carroll opened the stall, Rock On, located in a flea market at 93 Golborne Road, just off the Portobello Road in West London.

Dublin-born Carroll first entered the music business after swapping a model aircraft engine for a guitar in 1957: "I played rhythm guitar and bass in a few garage bands, including The Caravelles, [later to become The Greenbeats, the top Irish beat group in the 1960s]…. I was also promoting gigs—I'd been working in a bank but quit that in 1965 and went back into the music business on a full time basis."

After a spell managing and booking bands such as Rockhouse, The Uptown Band, The Method and Skid Row, as well as promoting bands including The Chieftains, The Nice and John Mayall's Bluesbreakers, Carroll moved to Bournemouth, England, and worked as a bus driver—all the while considering his next move:

Around this time, I discovered junk shops selling old 45s for shillings and started buying them for my own collection. Occasionally, you'd come across an old Chuck Berry 45 or Elvis HMV album which you knew weren't common. Then I discovered an ad in the back of *Melody Maker* for this magazine called *Record Mart* which contained listings of old records. I found a record I'd been looking for, for ages, "Mr Lee" by the Bobbettes [a 1957 hit], which was 17 shillings and sixpence, (just under one pound—three times the price of a single back then). That was the lynch pin, it was what pushed me into record dealing, if only in a small way.

A trip to America in 1970 proved more fortuitous. At the turn of the 1960s, the first stirrings of a new breed of pop 'archeologists'—people going to America to source records at company warehouses where they had lain neglected for years—began to emerge. Dealers would bring these back to Britain and advertise them in *Record Mart* and similar journals with quaintly snappy descriptions like "fantastic bopper", "hot guitar break", or "cat breaks up piano during middle eight!". Unfortunately, travelling to America in 1970 was not cheap (costing approximately £3,000 in today's terms). Luckily, on a holiday trip to Dublin, Carroll met the members of Skid Row (from who lead singer Phil Lynott had recently departed) and agreed to become their personal manager for an upcoming tour of America:

> While in America, I discovered that some of the record shops had oldies sections, stuff from the 1950s that was still in print… Joe Turner, The Coasters, Chuck Berry…. I discovered a copy of Charlie Gillett"s *The Sound of the City*, which was an incredible education. I found out about a huge number of records I'd not heard of, which had never been issued in England or were completely unknown…. We were kicking around in Boston for a week and listening to a fantastic oldies show on the radio every day from 12 until six in the afternoon. Plus there was an oldies shop… Big John's Oldies But Goodies Land, located on Washington Street in downtown Boston—the only exclusively oldies shop I came across in America. And I thought, London could do with one of these.

As Carroll's fascination with vintage vinyl swelled, his interest in Skid Row diminished somewhat. He did, however, get involved in the management of Lynott's new band Thin Lizzy, along with two other Dublin bands; Mellow Candle and Elmer Fudd (a band featuring guitarist Philip Donnelly, who went on to play with John Prine, Emmylou Harris and the Everly Brothers), all of which had a significant impact on the inception of Rock On:

> My stock was gleaned from junk and secondhand shops. But then I had a stroke of luck. Just before the stall was due to open we were in Ireland, Thin Lizzy were on a quick tour to replenish the coffers—and I discovered that the Decca distributor [Thin Lizzy were signed to Decca at this point] in Dublin had a room full of old London American 45s. So, I did a deal with them to cherry pick through those and bought about 1,800 for three and a half pence each, and some LPs, and came back and opened the stall. These London discs really kick-started the stall. I often had 50 copies of very rare records, like "Say Man" by Bo Diddley, and was able to sell them on for £1, even £2. Those 45s would be worth several thousand pounds now. Within two or three weeks of Rock On's launch, there'd be a queue of ten to 15 people waiting for me to open up in the morning. It was like bees round honey, a scrum of hands across the counter. It was the London 45s that attracted them…. The London label was the Holy Grail back then.

OPPOSITE CLOCKWISE FROM TOP:
Ted Carroll (far left) with the Caravelles, Dublin, 1960; Ted Carroll behind the counter at Rock On's Golbourne Road stall, circa 1980s. Image courtesy of Vicki Fox. Ted Carroll with Mellow Candle, 1970.

However, before long, Carroll found other sources for acquiring interesting records, including the newly opened Record and Tape Exchange in nearby Notting Hill, where customers were depositing their old mono albums, as the new stereo era rendered these potential treasures supposedly obsolete. He even acquired a stash of late 1960s 45s from a bicycle and pram shop in the Golborne Road. "That's the way records were sold back then", Carroll remembers:

> There was also a wholesale dealer of old 45s in New Jersey from whom I'd import up to 1,500 singles at a time, plus a guy—who's still going—who had a great record shop in Luton, FL Moore. He used to import ex-jukebox 45s from America and I would go up there once a week and I'd buy maybe 300 or 400 ex-jukebox singles for 10p each.

Other sources of old vinyl included Gibraltar and Malta (where British squadrons had once been stationed) and there were still dusty leftovers of the period, records which had been shipped out specifically for them. Nick Garrard—the former Meteors manager who still lives at Ace's old premises in Camden—was a teenager when he and his friends first started frequenting the market stall: "We lived by Heathrow—we'd come up to London, do the market (jumble sales, flea markets, etc) take them to Rock On and trade them for what Ted had. We were after the American 45s, Sun Records, whereas he wanted British label rock'n'roll like Frankie Lymon on Columbia. He'd swap us two Suns for one of those. We were 14, 15."

Brian Nevill, a long-time associate of Ace and its predecessors, remembers the stall in its earliest days:

> Something was in the air. I had a friend who lived in this flat in west London —a really vile, scruffy, horrible, bloke's flat—but the one thing pristine in this mess was a Dansette in mint condition and a bunch of records on the auto changer. And they were all vintage London records, which he'd bought the first time round. Thing was, this guy was playing these records in an un-ironic way, in 1972. And he wouldn't have parted with them, even though he was dirt poor. So I told him about Ted's stall, less than a minute's walk away. I remember the famous Elvis wallpaper and all these other stalls with their thin dividing walls, selling hippyish jewellery, retro clothing—and there, at the end of the row was a smelly, greasy caff—you'd go past the caff, and Ted had the whole back space, in an L-shape, with the stock behind the counter, belting out rock'n'roll and R&B at full blast.

Nevill became a regular customer, buying records he used to own and those that he missed. "Everyone was in a discovery mood—especially for rockabilly. We always knew that what we had was just the thin end of the wedge."

The reverberations of this period of revivalism were felt as far up as the Top 30 in the mid-1970s. Pop music was experiencing its first wave of self-rediscovery. From films such as *American Graffiti*, 1973, and David Essex's *That'll Be the Day*, 1973, retro rock'n'roll had become a highly fashionable option amid the prog and glam that prevailed in 1972 and 1974.

However, the increasing success of Rock On was a harbinger for the future, as opposed to a transient fad. As well as regular, obsessive collectors of rare rock'n'roll and subsequently R&B, rockabilly and northern soul, were customers who would later become significant figures in the punk era. (An era which, far from emerging out of the blue in 1976, had been gathering momentum for

some time; largely fuelled by an interest in rock'n'roll's 'basics', its roots and origins.) These included Malcolm McLaren, future manager of The Sex Pistols, Lenny Kaye (guitarist in The Patti Smith group) and Joe Strummer, years before he formed The Clash. In 1973, Phil Lynott would immortalise the stall in Thin Lizzy's "The Rocker": "I get my records from the Rock On stall/rock'n'roll/teddy boy, he's got them all...."

Come 1974, and Carroll decided to part ways with Thin Lizzy, following line-up problems with the band (though, before relinquishing his role as manager, he shepherded them onto a major label, Phonogram, from whence they hit the stratospheres of superstardom). Carroll's friend, Sylvia Keogh, who dealt in Victorian clothing, had asked him to share a stall with her in Soho Market in London's Chinatown. He subsequently decided to expand Rock On and asked an old friend, Roger Armstrong, if he might care to manage it. (It was arranged that Rock On occupied the premises Monday to Wednesday while Keogh traded Victorian goods from Thursday to Saturday.)

Along with a college acquaintance, Michael Clifford, Armstrong had formed a group called the Esoteric Music Society at Queen's University, who were later joined by Stan Brennan and Phil Gaston (both of whom also got involved in the Rock On empire). This rather solemn moniker initially disguised the activity of playing Mothers of Invention, The Velvet Underground and Pink Floyd albums, along with a smattering of oldies such as the Society's anthem "Daddy's Home" by Shep and the Limelites, in the student union attic. After stints in Dublin, working with The Chieftains, and later, Chips and Horslips, Armstrong went to London to manage a band called St James' Gate. Just as they disbanded, and while he was looking to enter the music business via a different route, he was approached by Carroll. "I was at a loose end trying to get into studios... when Ted asked me if I'd like to work his stall for three days a week. Well, it was wonderful for me, three days a week playing records, with more coming in all the time. Eight hours wasn't enough time to play them all."

Armstrong proved an enthusiastic and adept stall manager. He and co-stall worker, Gaston, spent a summer sawing wood and putting together boxes

OPPOSITE TOP TO BOTTOM:
Mellow Candle's *Swaddling Songs*, 1972, which is now extremely sought after, and Thin Lizzy's "The Rocker", 1973.

ABOVE LEFT TO RIGHT:
Ted Carroll with Thin Lizzy, circa 1970s, and the Rock On stall at Soho Market with Joe Strummer, Adrian Thrills and members of the Pop Group, early 1979. Photograph by Stephen Swan. Image courtesy of Daniel Swan.

for use on the stall, which would shortly become Rock On entirely. After the owner of Soho Market had offered the budding vinyl and antique clothing entrepreneurs two stalls for the price of one, Keogh moved into her own emporium.

By now, a palpable scene was beginning to develop—low budget, local, but fired up with the same essential, 'rough 'n' ready' real-time energies of early rock'n'roll. Because this scene flourished in pubs it acquired the slightly pejorative term of 'pub rock'. As Carroll reminisces:

> You had bands playing in pubs whose albums now change hands for hundreds of pounds. Charlie Gillett was playing a lot of old R&B, roots stuff, country; what you'd now call Americana, on his Radio London show—he was really quite influential. Then you had people like Brinsley Schwarz coming through the pubs (very much influenced by the band, Eggs Over Easy, who came from America), who really kicked things off by attracting considerable crowds to their residency at the Tally Ho pub in Kentish Town…. This became one of the first pub rock venues with Bees Make Honey, Kilburn & the High Roads and Ducks DeLuxe also commencing to play there.

There remained a thirst for rock'n'roll—past and present—to which the major record labels remained, if not oblivious, then certainly unaware of its scale and significance. "I remember in 1975—we had records that were underground hits like "Lights Out" by Jerry Byrne", recalls Carroll:

> You'd just sell as many copies as you could get your hands on. Then there was Hank Mizell's "Jungle Rock", which we sold by the dozen. We called Gusto Records in America, who owned the rights, but Charly Records, who'd been going for a while, had already licensed it from them and they went on to have

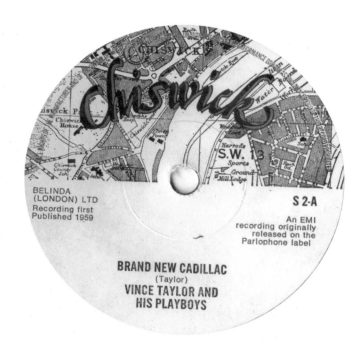

a huge number one hit with it. The first 'old' record we put out on Chiswick was "Brand New Cadillac" by Vince Taylor. We did well with it, because the shops were looking for something as a follow up to "Jungle Rock". We didn't chart but we got radio play and sold 10,000 copies pretty quickly.

It's no coincidence that this mood of revivalism coincided with punk's imminent moment of 'no future-ism'. "Rock'n'roll—when it hit in the mid-1950s—was like punk", says Carroll. "It was subversive, your parents hated it…. It didn't get played on the radio very much." By this time, the Rock On stock now included a considerable amount of 1960s British Beat Boom 45s for which a demand had rapidly increased. The Who were particularly popular, with mint copies of their debut single "I'm the Face" changing hands for up to £15 each (not cheap, bearing in mind that this was the early 1970s).

Initially, it seemed like rockabilly was going to be the new craze. Clubs such as The Bobby Sox Club at the White Horse pub in Willesden (where Crazy Cavan 'n' the Rhythm Rockers were "the first English British retro band to do rockabilly"), were on the upswing. When forming his first band, a young Shane MacGowan—an early Rock On stallfly who, according to Phil Gaston, "didn't look quite the full shilling, like he'd been sleeping in doorways, or whatever"—decided that rockabilly was where it was next at. "Younger kids were getting more into rockabilly and dumped the teddy boy thing—the teds became dinosaurs overnight", says Carroll.

However, it was punk that really kicked in, on a wave of gobbiness, and affectedly inept guitar anthems, inducing moral panic in its wake. While many in the rock establishment feared being swept into obsolescence, Rock On greeted the newcomers without demur. Among the other punk celebrities who would hang around at the Rock On stall in Soho were; The Damned, The Jam (who once put on an impromptu concert near the stall in the hope of getting arrested but, to their chagrin, failed to do so) and members of The Sex Pistols. New York's Ramones also looked in, seeking out the British bubblegum records they cited as an inspiration for "Blitzkrieg Bop", as well as fanzine writers like Mark Perry. And, recalls Carroll, the older guard occasionally turned up too:

OPPOSITE:
Ted Carroll—a typical day at Rock On, Camden, circa 1980s. Image courtesy of Roger Armstrong.

ABOVE:
Vince Taylor's "Brand New Cadillac"; the second single and first re-issue from Chiswick, 1976.

I remember Jimmy Page coming in with BP Fallon and buying a load of Sun 45s at the Golborne Road stall. Lemmy also used to visit regularly, John Peel would come in and lurk in the background… and then disappear, though he subsequently became a regular customer in Soho. Joe Strummer was in all the time. Jesse Hector—the main man of the Gorillas, one of the first bands we recorded—was there from day one. Chris O'Donnell, our booker for Thin Lizzy, would come in every Saturday morning. It was a social gathering; but doing business at the same time.

At the Soho stall, after the end of a day's business, instant decampment would take place at the Cambridge pub in Cambridge Circus off the Charing Cross Road. Fellow quaffers and holders-forth included a young, but very confident, Shane MacGowan (who later persuaded Stan Brennan, then managing the stall, to put up a notice saying "please don't dribble on the records"), as well as the staffers of the nearby Ray's Jazz shop in Shaftesbury Avenue and Dobell's music shop, in addition to a smattering of St Martin's students—all adding to the general mood of garrulous, cerebrally-charged hedonism.

By 1975, Carroll had opened a branch of Rock On in Camden Town, at Kentish Town Road, which made it extraordinarily central to Camden life—it was practically the first thing you saw when coming out of the station. The Camden shop was set up and run initially with a partner Barry Appleby, an original customer and Beach Boy fanatic, who would later open his own shop, Sea of Tunes, in nearby Buck Street.

Camden was to become, and remained for many years, the hub of the retro scene that became huge in the aftermath of punk, a sort of Postmodern explosion of former vintage styles which could be acquired cheaply and

developed—by the determinedly trendy with a fine disregard for the rather staid High Street youth fashions—into an idiosyncratic, 'pick 'n' mix' look of one's own. "It started with Camden Lock Market", says Vicki Fox, who began working at Rock On in 1978 and is now employed at Ace Records. "That brought people in wheeling, dealing, buying old clothes, books, records, old 1950s shoes, that retro look. Then other record shops opened up like Out on the Floor. Dingwalls was also very hip, with all the American acts coming in."

Rick Rogers, Chiswick's old press officer, had set up his own music PR business in a room above Holt's shoe shop next to Rock On. He initially managed The Specials, and set up their 2-Tone Records label, from these premises. The Rock On clientele was as mixed and dedicated as ever, from vinyl junkies who spent most of their wage packets on records, hip DJs, actors such as Jesse Birdsall (who had been known to spend £200 a time on vinyl sprees), music journalists like Nick Kent, Pete Silverton and Roy Carr; and the occasional heavyweight superstar hoving in from the firmament.

The Camden store eventually shut in the mid-1990s. Nick Garrard, who lived above the shop, managed it in its later years:

> In the last six months it only opened Saturdays and Sundays. We were winding it down. We were just selling what stock was left. So I'd do my morning stint at the post office, have a quick pint, then take the grilles down and work through till 6.30pm. We were still doing good business, right up to the end. Bob Dylan came in spent a load of money, mainly on Gospel albums. Same thing for The Cramps. They'd come in at six after we'd shut and stay for a couple of hours. It was 50/50 vinyl/CDs. So we did well. But you've got to consider rent, VAT, etc.

OPPOSITE:
Chiswick band, The Rings, jump outside Rock On in this lively publicity shot, circa 1970s.

ABOVE:
The Rock On shop, circa 1970s. Chiswick's original office was on the first floor and Ted Carroll's flat on the floors above. Image courtesy of Roger Armstrong.

FOLLOWING PAGES:
Vicki Fox behind the counter of the Rock On shop and filing records 1991. Image courtesy of Roger Armstrong. Advertisement for Rock On sale, circa 1970s.

Today, laments Fox, Camden is smarter, a great deal more expensive, but has largely dispensed with the elements upon which its reputation is based: "Rock On used to supply vinyl for the Hawley Arms, a real scummy, rocker's pub it was. Now that's been done out. All the drinking places are full of glass, steel bars and sofas. They've driven out the kind of people, the kind of places that made Camden vibey in the first place."

There is a tasteful odourlessness about twenty-first century record consumption, be it on CD, iPod or MP3. For Carroll, in those market stall years—during which the foundations were laid and the impetus was gathered for Chiswick, then Ace—the passion wasn't just for the music but for the sheer tactile joy of acquisition. In 1988, Carroll reminisced on some of his most memorable vinyl hunting exploits. Casting back to 1973, he recounts how he had managed to purchase some 1,300 ultra-rare 78 rpm platters for a bargain from the manageress of Mays for Music, an old music shop in Dublin that was in the process of closing down. On being told she had a store room full of old 78s she needed to get rid of, Carroll found himself flicking through a treasure trove of recordings by The Delmore Brothers, Wayne Raney, Hank Ballard & The Midnighters, Bill Doggett, The Lamplighters, Little Willie John and so forth. Being thankful to him for his 'altruism' she let him have the lot for £16. "I handed over the loot and, carefully packing the records, skipped out of the shop", says Carroll. "Some days you lose and some days you WIN!"

ABOVE CLOCKWISE FROM TOP LEFT:
Hank Ballard, circa 1960s, and Little Willie John, circa 1960s. Images courtesy of King Records, Inc. Wayne Rainey's *That Real Hot Boogie Boy*, 2002; and The Lamplighters' *Loving, Rocking, Thrilling*, 2005.

CHISWICK

CHISWICK

Brian Nevill, one-time employee of Rock On, and more recently consultant for Ace Records, was also a member of The Tooting Frooties—a band that played cheery, 'rough 'n' ready', old time rock'n'roll (as so many small outfits did in the mid-1970s, loudly yet largely unheard). Their one and only television appearance—on *Nationwide*, the British news and current affairs programme of the 1970s—came about after the band leader, Chris Barber, sourced a huge cache of 78s on the Savoy label. This vast find incurred the interest of *Nationwide's* researchers who asked Ted Carroll to find a contemporary rock'n'roll band to play live on the show as an adjunct to a discussion about the Savoy label, and the rock'n'roll revival in general. The band played, their performance cut to just under two minutes and, as Nevill relates ruefully, "it all went downhill for the Tooting Frooties after that".

Nonetheless, the event indicated Carroll's willingness to give new acts a stab at wider exposure. The Tooting Frooties used the basement in the Rock On shop for rehearsals. Among the other bands who shared the space were a rock'n'roll combo called The 101ers, led by a certain Joe Strummer. "It was a very fertile period, late 1974–1975", says Roger Armstrong:

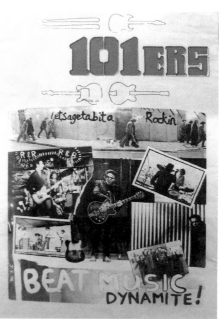

OPPOSITE LEFT TO RIGHT:

The Tooting Frooties performing
live with Brian Nevill on drums,
1976. Image courtesy of Brian Nevill.
Rare 101ers poster featuring
Joe Strummer, circa 1970s.
Image courtesy of Roger Armstrong.

BELOW LEFT TO RIGHT:

Early hand-drawn 101ers poster
while Marwood Chesterton aka
Mole was still in the group,
circa 1970s. Image courtesy of
Roger Armstrong. Ted Carroll's hand-
drawn advertisement for Vince
Taylor's "Brand New Cadillac", 1976.

There were great bands to see every night. I remember going out to see Little
Feat playing at the Rainbow supporting The Doobie Brothers, and the entire
venue emptying when Little Feat came off to go down the Hare and Hounds
where Brinsley Schwarz were playing. That was your double-header that night.
Quite quickly, Ted and I talked about starting up a little record label.

As far back as 1972, Carroll had hatched the notion of setting up a small
"boutique" label, as he describes it, in response to the many demands at the
stall for recordings such as Vince Taylor's "Brand New Cadillac", which weren't
just rare, but out of print altogether. He even approached Decca with the idea,
but other priorities, including his management of Thin Lizzy, meant that the
notion went into storage. By 1975, however, the sheer groundswell of activity
prompted his interest once again. "This was '75, before punk, before Stiff",
says Armstrong:

There had been a few indie labels but they'd come and gone. Then there were
things like Island—however, they had become quite major. But the idea of
a street level label, with no money behind it; that was something else. So we
decided to do it…. It wasn't people like Island or RAK who inspired us but
those like Chess and Sun and Modern from the 1950s.

Dr Feelgood were doing well at the time, there was a healthy rock'n'roll
scene, and at the stalls we were selling MC5, Stooges, New York Dolls and The
Flamin' Groovies. At a pop level were Showaddywaddy/Mud pop versions, all
a bit Butlins. We weren't pop producers, we worked with what we realistically

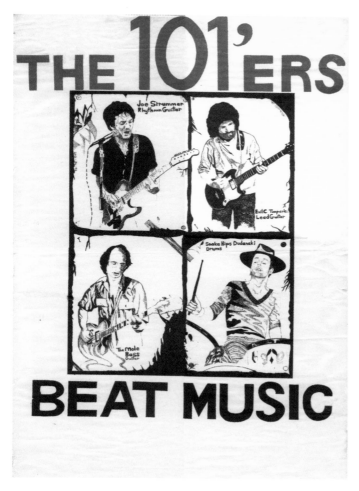

CHISWICK RECORDS "always a hit"

SW1 **	S4 *
Count Bishops Speedball E.P.	Gorillas
Route 66/Ain't Got You/Beautiful Delilah/	She's My Gal/Why Wait 'til Tomorrow
Teenage Letter	S5 *
S2 *	Count Bishops
Vince Taylor & The Playboys	Train Train/Taking It Easy
Brand New Cadillac/Pledging My Love	SW6 **
S3 *	Rocky Sharpe & The Razars E.P.
101'ers	Drip Drop/What's Your Name/So Hard To
Keys To Your Heart/5 Star Rock 'n' Roll	Laugh/That's My Desire
Petrol	SW7 **
	Little Bob Story E.P.
	I'm Crying/Come On Home/I Need Money/
	Cry Baby
	S8 *
	Gorillas
	Gatecrasher/Gorilla Got Me
	S9 *
	Radio Stars
	Dirty Pictures/Sail Away
	S10 *
	Radiators from Space
	Television Screen/Detective
	S11 *
	Skrewdriver
	You're So Dumb/I'm Crazy
	S12 *
	Count Bishops
	Baby You're Wrong/Stay Free
	S13 **
	Motorhead
	12" single

Chiswick, * 70p ** £1.00.

THE CHISWICK STAFF AT WORK

had to hand, understood, and could record for next to nothing. Those were the bands playing in the only venues available to them: pubs.

Going back to the 1950s, there have been musicians in this country playing old American music with verve and enthusiasm, and that's what these bands were doing. Some were good, some bad and some really great—we went in search of the latter.

The search very quickly yielded results. In mid-1975, they went to see a band called Chrome play at the Lord Nelson on Holloway Road. "Ted found them in the gig listing pages of *Melody Maker*", remembers Armstrong:

There were pages and pages of gigs listed, so we'd just go through the London section. Chrome looked like a good rock'n'roll name so we went to see them and they were all right…. By August of 1975 we had them in the studio… and, for about £120 at Pathway Studios, we made what became the "Speedball" EP with the band now called The Count Bishops.

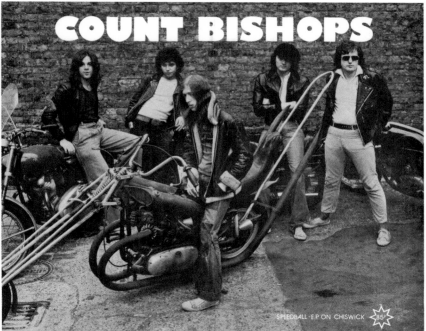

As Herb Fenstein later put it, the record's ensuing success indicated an appetite for "noisy, edgy white R&B that sounded like the first Rolling Stones album being played at 78 rpm". To produce the EP, the Rock On crew worked with Delga Press, a sleeve printer in South London; Hannibal, a label printer in Leicester, while lacquers were cut at Trident. "The blueprint for a thousand indie labels was born", declares Carroll.

"We didn't get the EP out till December 1975, presumably because we were new to the process", admits Armstrong:

> But at the same time, we were discovering that getting a record out wasn't this arcane, magical thing—it was pretty easy to get a record pressed—not rocket science. As the Desperate Bicycles (fanzine writers and band) famously said, it was easy, it was cheap, go do it. And that was the beauty of the 45 rpm format, of the record industry in those days—you could go out and do it with very little capital.

OPPOSITE LEFT TO RIGHT:

Chiswick "always a hit" flyer from June 1977, and Trevor Churchill, Dave Godin and Terry Chappell outside Soul City, Deptford High Street, circa 1966. Image courtesy of Norman Jopling.

ABOVE LEFT TO RIGHT:

The Count Bishops' "Speedball", 1975, the first 45 rpm 7" record on Chiswick. Image courtesy of Roger Armstrong. A rare poster featuring an alternative shot to the cover image on The Count Bishops' "Speedball" EP, 1975. Image courtesy of Roger Armstrong.

The music business, however, was not as straightforward. Armstrong and Carroll quickly realised that, while it was one thing to hammer out hot wax in the Holloway Road, it was quite another to negotiate the labyrinths and pitfalls of commerce. Enter Trevor Churchill, who had also previously worked at Rock On. "Trevor had gone off to a [music industry] job in Germany", says Armstrong:

> And before he'd left we'd told him we'd like him to work with us, on the basis that we needed a record company guy—for your accounting, your back end, your royalties—certain knowledge you needed to become a record company, which was a bit more complex than just making a record. After some back and forth he came on board as the first employee of Chiswick Records.

Chiswick (a tongue in cheek homage to London Records) was incorporated through a company Churchill had formed, but left on the shelf as a contingency, as he moved between jobs. Churchill had first met Carroll after selling him

VARIOUS ARTISTS
Submarine Tracks and Fool's Gold/Chiswick Chartbusters Volume One. (Chiswick)

"THEY SAY love can move a mountain, love's gone in our teens . . ."The 101'ers' Joe Strummer howls with strangled larynx over the "Jumping Jack Flash" derived riff that the band's finest moment is built around, their Juke Box Classic entitled "Keys To Your Heart".

"Joe used to come into the shop all the time," says Chiswick's Ted Carroll in reference to his *real* record shop, Rock On in Soho, the temple that Chiswick Records evolved from. "I went along to see 101'ers and they were at the stage that's best for a band — hungry, on their way up, fresh, full of enthusiasm and total energy. By the time they reach the Hammersmith Odeon level, a band has lost something."

Chiswick Records, born Summer '75, used imagination instead of old sales figures. They were a direct reaction against the giant record company corporations in much the same way as the Pistols were a direct reaction against the dinosaur bands of the sixties.

Along with Stiff Records, Chiswick has been largely responsible for the resurgence of the quality rock single (usually lovingly picture-sleeve packaged) aimed at a neglected section of youth. Chiswick thought that putting out records should be about music, not product, that sales should be earned on merit, not reputation. Hey, Ted Carroll and his partner Roger Armstrong must be crazy bastards, right?.

Wrong, kid. This superb anthology modestly subtitled "Chiswick Chartbusters Volume One" is £2.25 cheap and living proof that good guys win. A dozen tracks in all, the 101'ers open the show with the stuttered chording of "Keys To Your Heart", a quintessential recording for any of you troops interested in seeing where The Clash grew from, dateline early last year, pre.Sex Pistols

Chiz Chiz: Nigel Molesworth plays guitar aka JOE STRUMMER in the pre-Clash 101'ers

Hi! I'm Jesse Hector of The Gorillas

CHISWICKED!

satori and the gathering storm clouds.

There are also three songs from the only true inheritors of the legacy left by the Small Faces, the band who warranted a stream of hit singles, Jesse Hector's vision of London Mod omnipotence — The Gorillas!

Note the superb early '77 single "Gatecrasher", its addictive riff slashed out with good natured malevolence by Hector, also the intoxicated raunch of the tribute to the chicklet of your heart, "She's My Gal", and the echoed repetition of the Skinhead moonstomp-flavoured "Gorilla Got Me."

There's a brace of Le Havre rivvum 'n' blooze tracks from Little Bob Story, the frantic chord changes of lost-lust frustration in "I'm Crying", and the comparatively sedate "Baby Don't Cry", both of them recorded in December 1976.

The Count Bishops have a trilogy of cuts that include their junk-sick paen to obsessive sexual craving, "Train Train", when the girl you need ain't around, and the ones that *are* around just ain't good enough. Their best song and Love psychosis incarnate.

The Bishops' other two songs are the Chuck duck-walk derived "Teenage Letter" (the absorption and expression of influences works), and that boring old warhorse "Route 66" which has an effect similar to swallowing all your Mum's National Health valium.

Rocky Sharpe And The Razors evoke the emotion and imagery of beautiful self-pitying *American Graffiti* Rock Dreams for lost teenage angels with "Drip Drop" and "So Hard To Laugh".

Which leaves the acceptable face of the Page Three mentality, "Dirty Pictures" by the Radio Stars. Chuckling pop meets a parody of nasty New Wave with its flies undone and lines like *"I get my kicks up in the attic, with a Kodak Instamatic"* and other such nonsense.

"Yeah, the big companies took a while to catch on that something new was happening," Chiswick's Ted Carroll says, "and then they went apeshit. Sometimes I think it'll kill it. Then some unknown kid walks into the shop with some new band's amazing tapes and it all seems worthwhile."

Rock on, Chiswick.
Tony Parsons

a vast amount of his extensive collection, made up largely of old soul records. As a child, the former had been an avid music fan—however his particular interest, somewhat unusually, was how record companies were run. Some kids yearned to pick up a guitar, Churchill yearned to pick up a ledger: "The interaction between the companies, who was licensing what to whom, was fascinating to me."

Although a music lover and serious collector, Churchill had become rather disaffected with music in the late 1960s and early 70s. He worked at both Motown's British office and at the label set up by the Rolling Stones, but found very little he considered worthy of signing. He had passed on a Roxy Music demo, but doesn't regret the decision: "Everybody heard that demo as it did the rounds. It was abysmal." The group, Queen, was also pitched to him: "Pre-punk was about 'how powerful is the manager?'." I had Queen's manager come in—they had the full package—when I was working for the Rolling Stones. But there was no way the deal would have fitted—the Stones were on a licensing deal anyway."

However, Churchill did know about hit singles—during his stint at EMI as manager of the Bell label, he scored a big one with Edison Lighthouse's "Love Grows (Where My Rosemary Goes)" and, of course, his knowledge of business matters was wide-ranging. And so, it mattered little that Churchill had never really been interested in British music generally, let alone the burgeoning class of 1975. "Fortunately, Ted and Roger were", he says:

They were out at the pubs every night. Musically, Chiswick was of no interest to me whatsoever. I was into the first phase of rock'n'roll and soul but, by the 1970s, even soul had very little interest for me. It was too clean, too produced— and then it turned into disco and that was that, as far as I was concerned! It

OPPOSITE:

The guitars of Nigel Molesworth and Jesse Hector clash in an *NME* review of *Fool's Gold*, 6 August 1977.

ABOVE:

Bell's Cellar of Soul: Vol 1, compiled by Trevor Churchill in 1968.

was good because it meant that I could get on with business while Ted and Roger could get on with their side of things unfettered.

Churchill's contacts at EMI were also handy when it came to licensing old records, which was part of Chiswick's Janus-faced remit—looking to the past as well as the future. "We knew that one of the most in-demand rock'n'roll records of that time was "Brand New Cadillac" by Vince Taylor", says Armstrong: "Because we were selling any copies we could get for very high prices. So, using Trevor's contacts, we licensed the track off EMI. We couldn't have done that without Trevor. Nowadays, it's harder to license from majors because they want to do it themselves."

However, it was the new wave (or, strictly speaking, pre-new wave) of rockers who were beginning to generate press excitement—with Pete Silverton at Sounds, among others, providing support in the face of what Armstrong describes as the "yes obsessives" who still dominated the music press. Joe Strummer's The 101ers were coaxed into the studio for a session, the result of which was "Keys To Your Heart". Strummer's choppy, combative guitar style and hoarse vocals only hint at the insurrectionary force he would pilot with The Clash. "Actually, there was as much, if not more, politics about The 101ers as there was with The Clash", remarks Armstrong: "Again, they get called a pub rock band but it's a different strain, they were more a squatter band, they came from a more hippy thing. There was a real individuality about them, they weren't so self-consciously retro R&B. They were more shambolic, especially early on."

"A lot of guys came through our doors in those days—Jim Kerr for instance, as Johnny from Johnny and The Self Abusers, who of course went onto big things with Simple Minds", Carroll recalls.

The band were obviously worried that they might not be taken seriously with that name and they rang up about three weeks before the record was due for release and asked if they could change it. I asked what the new name was and

ACE RECORDS

when they said, The Simple Minds, I said: 'No, it's too late.' It wasn't, but we already had orders for about 1,500 copies because many shops thought that the name was hilarious and had ordered several copies on that basis.

However, there was one artist both Carroll and Armstrong agreed was going to be a star—Joe Strummer. As Armstrong recalls:

> It was a funny mixture with him—a bit of charisma, a lot of passion. I'd seen him playing in a pub in Elgin Avenue. They were pretty anarchic then. Then Ted saw them at Dingwalls a little while later and they'd tightened up into this great unit. Ted came to the stall the next morning—he's not normally that excitable—and says: 'I've just seen this kid, and he's an absolute star.'

Chiswick's next signing was The Gorillas (formerly The Hammersmith Gorillas), led by an extraordinarily extroverted Jesse Hector, a scrawny riot of loud check flares, two tone shoes and mutton chop whiskers. Hector was certainly bursting with ambition. "It's quite simple", he said of himself in an *NME* interview in 1977. "I'm special. Very soon the kids are going to rely on me the way they once did on Jagger, Townshend and Hendrix. New stars must emerge, and I know I'm the logical successor." Certainly, with the strafing sonics of "Gorilla Got Me", they were a more ambitious proposition than some of their contemporaries. "Jesse, the lead singer, was one of the most amazing stage performers you ever saw, you couldn't keep your eyes off him", says Armstrong. "Hanging from the ceiling by his toenails, playing guitar with his teeth, that sort of thing. He was extreme rock'n'roll—even the punks liked him. *Sniffin' Glue* put him on their front cover."

Chiswick, as Carroll rightly boasts, had created a template for indie labels such as Stiff and Rough Trade—where the onus was not merely about shifting units but attempting to do so with a certain style and aesthetic. This was key to punk's DIY narrative, and widely emulated over the next few years across Britain, from Factory in Manchester to Postcard in Scotland, Zoo in Liverpool

OPPOSITE CLOCKWISE FROM TOP LEFT:
Vince Taylor card, 1976, and the back and front covers of Johnny and The Self Abusers' "Saints & Sinners/Dead Vandals", 1977.
Image courtesy of Roger Armstrong.

ABOVE LEFT TO RIGHT:
Front and back cover of The 101ers' "Keys To Your Heart", 1976.
Image courtesy of Roger Armstrong.

THE RISE AND DEMISE OF THE 101ERS.

In late 1974 the 101ers commenced their career at the Chippenham
public house near Ladbroke Grove. This pub was the scene of many
wild nights during the weeks that followed as the 101ers established themselves as the favourite local band. Word of the 101ers'
high energy approach to rock'n'roll and of the crazed antics of
their front man, Joe Strummer, soon spread through the London
pub circuit and by the Summer of 1975 the band was playing pubs
all over the city as well as being much in demand for benefits and
free concerts.
The press began to take notice and a string of rave "Caught in the
Act" reviews meant that the band had no difficulty in moving onto
the College circuit in the autumn. At this stage, financial help
either from a large record company or a wealthy manager,was
essential, but not forthcoming. The band continued to slog up
and down the country borrowing or hiring vans and equipment but
gradually their determination and will to survive was eroded and
the frustration caused by this situation began to create internal
friction which led to the break-up a few weeks ago. The 101ers
brought a lot of people a great deal of pleasure during the course
of their short career. Their highly energetic and basic approach
to the music they played was the essence of what rock'n'roll is
all about.
Shortly before they broke up, Chiswick managed to lure the 101ers
into the studio where they recorded one of their own compositions
in the first take. We feel that this example of the 101ers unsoph-
isticated but exciting style of music makes a great single, which
despite the demise of the band, deserves to see the light of day.
We hope that you agree withus.

Footnote Happily we hear that Joe Strummer ex-101ers vocalist,
rhythm guitarist and human dynamo has joined a new band "The
Heartdrops" who will be making their debut in a few weeks time.
Don't miss them.

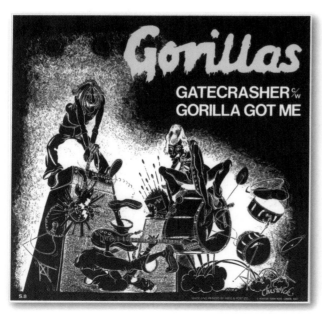

and so forth. It saddened Armstrong, therefore, that punk's emerging major players all chose to sign with the bigger labels. The old manager-as-driver syndrome that Churchill had noted in the early 1970s, still held sway, it seems.

"The Damned went to Stiff—I always say, because I went on holiday", jokes Armstrong:

> Bernie [Rhodes], who managed The Clash, and Malcolm [McLaren], who had The Pistols; they never had any intention of going independent [either], they didn't want to know. They wanted to go take as much money off a major record company as possible. It's ironic really that, in the middle of what was an independently generated scene that the major record companies initially despised, the major bands like The Clash all wanted to be on major record labels.

Unlike most of the other indie labels of the time, Chiswick did not focus on just one style of music. The records that came out in the first three years of its history ranged from British R&B, to heavy metal, power pop, punk, rockabilly and a worldwide hit with an AOR (adult orientated rock) track. Chiswick releases generated excitement, not least because—anticipating Ace's later 'all round package' philosophy when it came to putting out records—they came with all the trimmings so beloved of collectors; picture sleeves, badges, coloured vinyl, even slogans.

One key signing in 1977, was Motorhead, led by ex-Hendrix roadie, and erstwhile Hawkwind member, Lemmy. Though Chiswick were avowedly anti-heavy metal, Motorhead were the exception in that regard; their minimal, speed-driven guitar thrash distinguishing them from the poodle-haired, fussy soloing tendencies of other metal. In their own way, they fit comfortably within Chiswick's roster of rock'n'rollers, and punks.

Lemmy had been one of Carroll's earliest customers at Rock On in 1971, seeking out copies of no frills 1960s rock groups like The Primitives and The Birds. In 1975, he was thrown out of Hawkind, having been found in possession of a few grams of 'biker speed'. Fired up by the likes of The Primitives, however, he resolved to start a new band which would be "very basic… loud, fast, city, raucous, arrogant, paranoid, speed-freak rock'n'roll". The Carpenters, it

OPPOSITE CLOCKWISE FROM TOP:
"The Rise and Demise of the 101ers" press release, circa 1970s; Ted Carroll posing in a promotional shot with The Gorillas, circa, 1970s; and The Gorillas' "Gatecrasher/Gorilla Got Me", 1977.

ABOVE:
Motorhead promotional shot, circa 1970s.

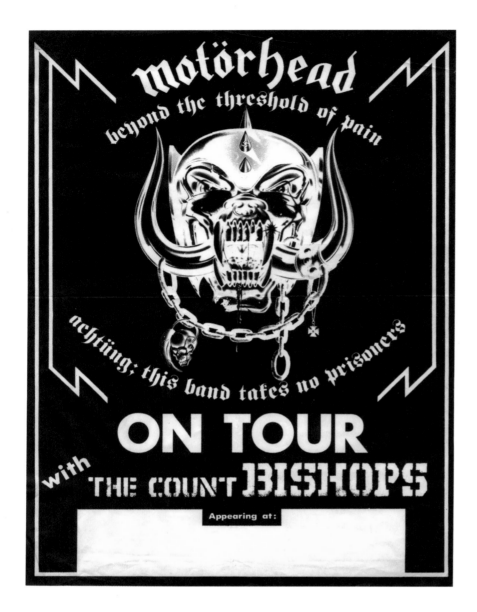

seemed, was not quite what he had in mind. Recording with the musician, Dave Edmunds, he produced an album for United Artists that was beset by line-up problems. After the company decided not to release the LP, he was forced to rely on the hospitality of the Hells Angels as he contemplated his next step.

Despite having finally managed to put together the best ever Motorhead line up, Lemmy, and other members of the group, decided to throw in the towel. Lemmy approached Armstrong at the stall to inform him of the news, and said that they were hoping to record a live LP before breaking up. Armstrong suggested that he contact Carroll. As Carroll recalls:

> Lemmy called me to say that they were breaking up and that Doug Smith had agreed to front £250 towards the cost of the Rolling Stones mobile and could we help. His plan was to record Motorhead's final gig about three weeks later at The Marquee. As a suitable date at the Marquee could not be arranged for a couple of months, it was decided to record a single, for instant release. The band left London a week or so later and drove down to the Escape Studios in Kent, where they were booked in for two days.

ABOVE:
Poster for Motorhead and The Count Bishops tour, circa 1970s.

OPPOSITE CLOCKWISE FROM TOP LEFT:
Rocky Sharpe & The Replays at Rock On Camden, circa 1970s; Radio Stars promotional shot, circa 1970s; and Sniff 'n' the Tears' "Driver's Seat", 1978, Chiswick's biggest worldwide hit record.

Carroll arrived the next evening, to find Lemmy in the vocal booth adding the finishing touches to the vocal on "City Kids". A quick listen to monitor mixes revealed that something quite unique had happened during the intervening 20 hours. All the frustration and anger over the past year's hang ups, the record company rejections, the continual put downs, the bad press, the shoe string finances, had been poured into the 16 track tapes at Escape Studios.

"What do you think", enquired Lemmy quietly as the last echoes of the final track died away and the wooden barn that housed the Studios stopped vibrating. "Well, I think you'd better get on and finish the album" Carroll replied; still reeling from the full volume playback.

Motorhead did go some way to living up to Chiswick's hope that it would be the "fastest, loudest, dirtiest album of all time". The title track, backed by "City Kids" was also released on 12", hitherto a format generally only used for disco 45s, but which maximised the volume generated by Lemmy and the rest of the band. The sales the single generated would have seen it ride high in today's Top 30, but in 1977 it only peaked at number 51.

At this stage, however, Chiswick were under no illusions that they could hold onto Motorhead—the deal had been for one album only and such was the low budget structure of small indie labels, that they could not realistically expect to provide the band the financial boost necessary to take them to the next stage. And so, after a period of hesitancy on the part of the major labels, the group eventually moved to the Bronze label.

Come 1978, Chiswick still had the capacity to sneak out the odd hit. "We had our punk stuff, much of which wasn't going to be massively successful: too off the wall", admits Armstrong. "We had Radio Stars, who were punky power pop. They had a Top 20 hit with "Nervous Wreck". We had "Driver's Seat" by Sniff 'n' the Tears, a strange record to make in the middle of punk. And we had Rocky Sharpe & The Replays doing "Rama Lama Ding Dong" which was a chart success."

Radio Stars

Chiswick
3 KENTISH TOWN ROAD LONDON N W 1

"Rama Lama Ding Dong" was indeed a huge hit, an immaculate piece of rock'n'roll which, while hardly heralding a new rock dawn, was faithful right down to the last doo-wop and sold well to the type of audience who lapped up the likes of The Darts in droves. Churchill, who at the time had little involvement with repertoire matters, had been responsible for signing the group.

Rocky Sharpe & The Replays were initially Rocky Sharpe and the Razors, a ten piece, Brighton based, rock'n'roll revival outfit inspired to some extent by Sha Na Na. The group rapidly became very popular in the pubs and colleges of London, but were unable to get a record deal and broke up in 1976. Out of the ashes emerged The Darts who quickly scored a record deal and went on to major success with an act and material based on the original Razors model.

Sharpe and his brother, Jan, continued pursuing their individual careers (in acting and photography) until that fateful call from Chiswick Records. Churchill had been listening to the Razors' EP, an early release on Chiswick (which consisted of recordings paid for by a fan and leased to Chiswick after the original band had broken up). Impressed by Sharpe's fabulous vocals, and on seeing the success that had been achieved by The Darts, Churchill suggested that Chiswick do a single with the singer. He also suggested a remake of "Rama Lama Ding Dong" and brought in Pete Wingfield as producer.

The rest is pop history. "Rama Lama Ding Dong", the remake, became a Top 20 hit in Britain and was even more successful across Europe—selling over half a million copies. Sharpe and his brother formed a group, along with bass singer, Mike Vernon, and vocalist, Helen Highwater, to exploit the record and several successful follow ups. The group went on to score seven hit singles and recorded three albums before disbanding in 1984.

It was here that Churchill's record business experience paid dividends. For each territory, he negotiated individual licensing deals. As he explains: "That means that if you get a hit in, say, Spain, it doesn't have to be cross-collateralised.

OPPOSITE:
Radio Stars poster for "Dirty Pictures" featuring Martin Gordon's then girlfriend and some over excited band members, 1977.

ABOVE LEFT TO RIGHT:
Sniff 'n' The Tears' *Fickle Heart*, 1978, and Rocky Sharpe & The Replays' *Rama Lama*, 1979.

It wouldn't count against having a flop with the same single in France—the advance there may be unrecouped. Those advances saw Chiswick through the late 1970s."

Meanwhile, in Britain, Chiswick approached Colin Burn at EMI and arranged a licensing deal:

> They had this licensing division in Thayer Steet, away from the Manchester Square building. It was a lovely atmosphere, there was Fantasy (Records), Motown, all going on there under the same roof; we all got on well. We had a great label manager there, Martin Barter, who really got involved with what we were doing and was most helpful.

However, while this happy arrangement serviced Rocky Sharpe with a hit, the same could not be said of Sniff 'n' the Tears. Despite their punkish moniker, they were a rather poppy proposition, with their discreet synthesised flourishes, finely turned hooks and un-abrasive vocals and lyrics. "Driver's Seat", released in 1978, could and should have been a major pop hit; a key fixture in all our listening yesteryears. Overseas, it was. In Britain, however, it stalled. "It was rotten luck on our part", recalls Armstrong:

> It had just reached 42 in the chart when the big boys round the corner stole the sales force. The [EMI] sales force had just blown it on Kate Bush and Queen and they needed to get hits with the next ones. So the rug was pulled from under our feet, the record dropped in the charts the next week—we were furious. Internal EMI politics wrecked it for us. I always think that was a big turning point for us because if that record had taken off in Britain, the whole future might have changed for us.

An album, however, was eventually licensed to Atlantic in America where "Driver's Seat" became a Top 20 hit. Undeterred for the time being, Chiswick took up their second chance to sign The Damned, who had just fallen out with Stiff and been, as Armstrong puts it, "kicked out the door in a very public and offensive and unnecessary way (not that The Damned were exactly shrinking violets)".

Even Churchill, though hardly a fan of punk, saw the simple logic in bringing The Damned on board when he saw 2,500 fans crammed into the Lyceum going loudly ape for the group. "The Damned were Roger's indulgence", remarks Vicki Fox. "They were his babies."

Always a fan of The Damned, Armstrong could see that, by 1979, they were "the unhippest thing in the universe". Combustible and rambunctious—he also knew they would be a handful. However, there was more to The Damned musically than they were often given credit for. They debuted on Chiswick with the 7" tornado that was "Love Song", which reached number 20 in the charts and saw Captain Sensible debut his furry "okapi" suit on *Top of the Pops*. Buoyed by this success, Chiswick agreed to do an album with them, which Armstrong co-produced with the band. Once more this demonstrated that, beneath their exterior of daft get-up, studio prankery and drunken episodes, The Damned were taking their music a good deal more seriously. However, what Armstrong has called "the luck of The Damned" struck when their follow-up single "Smash It Up" was banned by the BBC, on the grounds that the title represented an incitement to violence.

ABOVE:
"Smash It Up" sticker.

OPPOSITE CLOCKWISE FROM TOP LEFT:
Rat Scabies (drums); Captain Sensible (guitar); Algy Ward (bass); and Dave Vanian (vocals) of The Damned, circa 1970s.

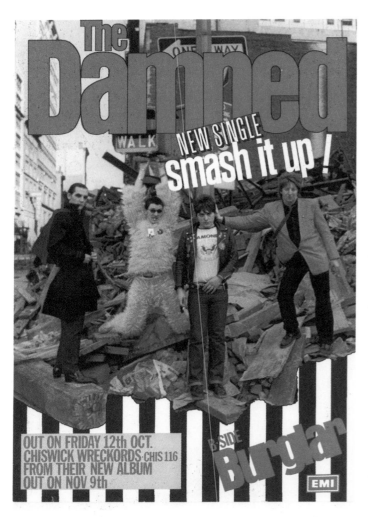

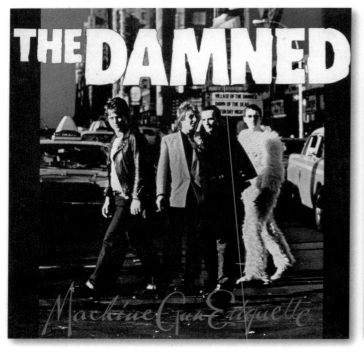

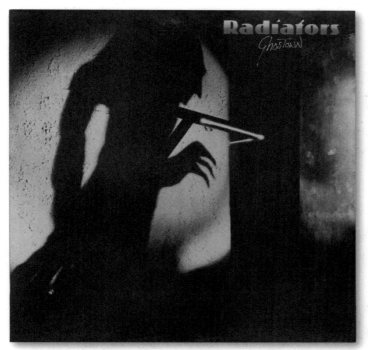

The album, *Machine Gun Etiquette*, performed well in the charts but was
followed by a drunken appearance on the *Old Grey Whistle Test* involving
a malfunctioning organ being thrown at a cameraman, then a confrontation
with a mob-connected promoter in Italy—all of which made the voyage of The
Damned a boisterous and unpredictable one. Armstrong looked in on them
as they recorded their second album in Wales, only to find himself having to
sidestep a pool of sick outside the studio and bass player Paul Gray storming
out as he quit the band. (This turned out to be an elaborate prank typical of
the band.) Still, *The Black Album*, the resultant LP, did much to scotch The
Damned's reputation as a joke outfit. However, they were not making good
on their advance. Rat Scabies' father had taken over as manager and Captain
Sensible was rather bitter about Chiswick's plans to release a series of singles
from *The Black Album*. "We had a good run with them", says Armstrong:

> But, by the second album, they became very difficult. They kept changing
> managers—I was doing stuff with them that was managerial, which made for a
> terrible conflict with the record label job. The relationships weren't happy and
> there were various other substances which didn't help—so eventually I had to
> say voluntarily, look guys, if you can find yourselves another deal, we'll let you
> go. [Which they did and eventually went onto Bronze, and subsequently, MCA.]

The Radiators were another should-have-been for Chiswick. *TV Tube Heart*—
their first album for the label—had been a robust enough affair; a concept
album based on the social effects of television. For their second, *Ghostown*,
Tony Visconti was brought in. He worked the band up to a highly finished
product, emphasising their melody and Beatles-like versatility and idealism.
However, what was perceived as a change of musical direction did not go down
well with their traditional punk following, as they discovered to their utter
chagrin when supporting Stiff Little Fingers at London's Electric Ballroom.

Philip Chevron, the band's lead man, was so saddened that they would not play another British gig for over 25 years. Moreover, Chiswick simply weren't in the position to give the album the sort of push it needed to be the commercial proposition it deserved to be. The album was fairly well received but didn't take. "I love *Ghostown*", said Chevron many years later. "It stands up very well, and I think it's still got hidden depths. It yearns for a changed society, so it's always going to resound." Carroll did give Chevron a job in Rock On, where he remained until he joined The Pogues.

"Today, *Ghostown* is considered a huge record in Ireland, spoken of in the same breath as *Pet Sounds* and *Astral Weeks*", says Armstrong. "The Radiators started off as Ireland's premier punk band, very influential on U2, say. So when U2 played Croke Park a while back, the Radiators re-formed to open for them and U2 paid them a substantial sum of money which wasn't needed—it was sort of a thank you for what The Radiators had done for them."

There were inevitably occasions when bands became disgruntled with the commercial scope they could expect from Chiswick. Says Charlie Gillett: "After Chiswick did the deal with EMI, particularly with Sniff 'n' the Tears, there were other band managers who insisted that their groups be treated on the same basis as if they were on EMI themselves. Whereas, the truth was, these were bands that only Chiswick would have picked up in the first place—EMI never could have."

Shane MacGowan's first 'punkabilly' band, The Nips, certainly had high hopes when they signed to the label. In Carol Clerk's *Pogue Mahone: Kiss My Arse: The Story of the Pogues*, The Nips' then manager Phil Gaston explains:

> We went to Ted and Roger because we trusted them. We didn't know our way around the big, huge companies. We knew that if we went to any of the major labels, we wouldn't be able to stay in the picture; we didn't have the clout. Chiswick put out "Gabrielle" as a single, but they weren't the kind of people who spent a lot of money on promotion and placement. They weren't a chart record company. They were just the same as us, only bigger. If we'd been lucky and had a hit with that, everything in the garden would've been rosy, but the whole deal with Chiswick was then called into question.

In truth, "Gabrielle" is hardly punkabilly but rather a tentatively respectable stab at polished new wave, with MacGowan displaying an impressive vocal range of grimaces, pleas and sneers. However, the single flopped and MacGowan was extremely pissed off. In an interview, he at once dismissed "Gabrielle" as a "dumb, stupid love song" while churlishly excoriating his former label. Speaking to *ZigZag* in 1980, he exclaimed: ""Gabrielle" is a good tune, but Chiswick fucked it up and I am fucking ashamed to have been associated with a silly pop record."

As the 1980s dawned, Chiswick could boast a genuinely diverse and interesting roster. There was Albania, who Armstrong knew from Belfast days, who proposed a cultural alliance with Europe's pariah nation, and whose music anticipated—far too soon for their own commercial good—the sort of pan-European musical eclecticism that would become more commonplace decades later.

There were The Meteors, formidable precursors of the 1980s psychobilly fixation whose "Radioactive Kid" was a bullet-hard fusion of punk and

OPPOSITE:
Radiators/Johnny Moped Roundhouse poster for the recording of the aborted *Sound of Music* LP, circa 1970s.

ABOVE:
The Nips 'n' Nipple Erectors' *Bops, Babes, Booze & Bovver*, 1987.

rockabilly's dementedly raw directness. There were Two Two, a couple of nicely scrubbed up would-be synth-popsters, who could easily have given Wham! or Spandau Ballet a run for their money (and whose "Kwagayo" sounds as busily, infectiously funky now as it did then). And Jakko, a virtuoso jazz guitarist of Polish extraction, whose "Grab What You Can" could be characterised as resembling a more soulful Duran Duran.

However, by now, the writing was on the wall. The music scene had moved on. Punk had evolved in multiple directions, from the rarefied realms of post-punk experimentalism, to the canny, colourised opportunism of new pop (ABC, The Associates). Moreover, despite the impact of indie labels like Chiswick, Stiff and Rough Trade, more than a shoestring budget was required to tie up a hit single. As a series of worthy commercial failures had indicated, it required a much bigger budget in this coming day and age to crash the Top 40. And, with the era of videos and MTV just around the corner, hitmaking would once again become more or less the sole preserve of the corporate labels. "Everything went back into the hands of the big record companies", says Vicki Foxx. "It reverted to big business. Acceptability; always a bad thing. Ted and Roger were always good at giving people a break, a bit of recording time…. but they couldn't do huge, full page ads." Ever the shrewd businessman, Churchill anticipated that Chiswick's days were numbered—they would have to wind down or face the fate that eventually befell some of their contemporaries. "It was a clear decision", says Churchill:

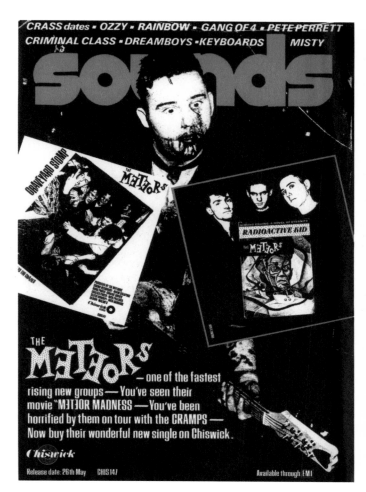

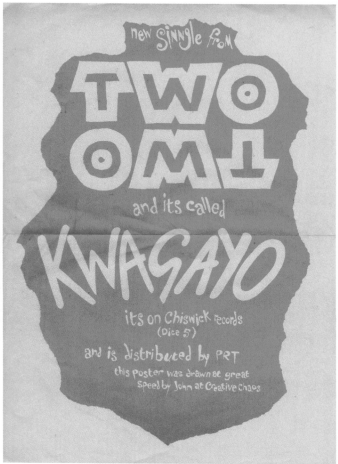

There was no question we had to make it. This was a time when you could make no kind of headway in getting a hit unless you put big money into videos. Stiff was a good example of how we could have ended up—overspending on marketing and it doesn't happen, it all ends in tears. I know Stiff is revered but as a well-run establishment it was not so good.

Churchill was resolute to learn from his own father's business experience:

He was a mad designer, determined to make the perfect vacuum cleaner. But he had no idea how to run a business, he hated his accountants, his bankers. I remember thinking, I don't want that to happen to me. Let's work things out, let's make clear, conscious decisions. It was worse for Roger, because those bands were his, and he must have been bitterly upset. As for Ted and I, we just wanted to make the right decision and sell records.

However, Armstrong puts up no argument against the decision today:

By the time we'd turned into the 1980s, it was men with funny haircuts and strange trousers playing ironing boards. We tried to move with these times ourselves with Jakko, a fabulous, jazz rock guitar player, which is probably what he should have stuck to. We had Two Two, a boy band duo, a year before Wham!. Again, good pop records—but they didn't have the whole shuttlecocks down the trousers thing going on, they were a bit more rough and ready. But there's always been that thing with us. We were good at starting people's careers,

OPPOSITE:
The Nips promotional shot, circa 1970s.

ABOVE LEFT TO RIGHT:
Front cover of *Sounds*, which was used to make this poster for the new Meteors single, circa 1970s, and a Two Two poster, circa 1970s. Image courtesy of Roger Armstrong.

be it Joe Strummer, Jim Kerr, Kirsty MacColl [who started life with the racy and very un-MacColl-like Drug Addix].

The bottom line is, our failure to have massive success is our success. If you look at someone like U2 at Island, who've become huge, you build a company around that act, to support it. And when that huge act isn't recording, you've got this huge system in place and you've got to feed it something. So you go out and make more and more records. And they're not all U2, they're not all huge. And you spend money on acts that aren't successful and you end up spending your profit. It ends up altering the kind of company you are.

Chiswick had certainly stretched themselves, despite the grumblings of one or two of their acts. Armstrong recalls the agonies suffered, for example, during the later recording sessions by The Radiators, in which they really pushed out the production boat. "Trevor was having kittens in the corner", he remembers:

In the space of seven, eight years we'd gone from raw, visceral rock'n'roll to places like Townhouse, using multiple studios, making epic pop with Hans Zimmer, learning production at the controls. It didn't work, so we quit. We had one last flourish with Rocky Sharpe [with "Shout! Shout!"]—a big, dumb record that was a huge hit, which brought us back full circle.

Fortunately, however, Armstrong, Churchill and Carroll had Ace up their sleeve. The future was the past. They came full-circle, having met through their mutual passion for old records, they translated that into the next phase of their business. Now they could concentrate on music they really knew about and understood.

ABOVE LEFT TO RIGHT:
Front cover of The Drug Addix'
"The Drug Addix Make a Record", 1978.
Image courtesy of Roger Armstrong.
Rocky Sharpe & The Replays' *Shout!*
Shout! (second cover), 1981.

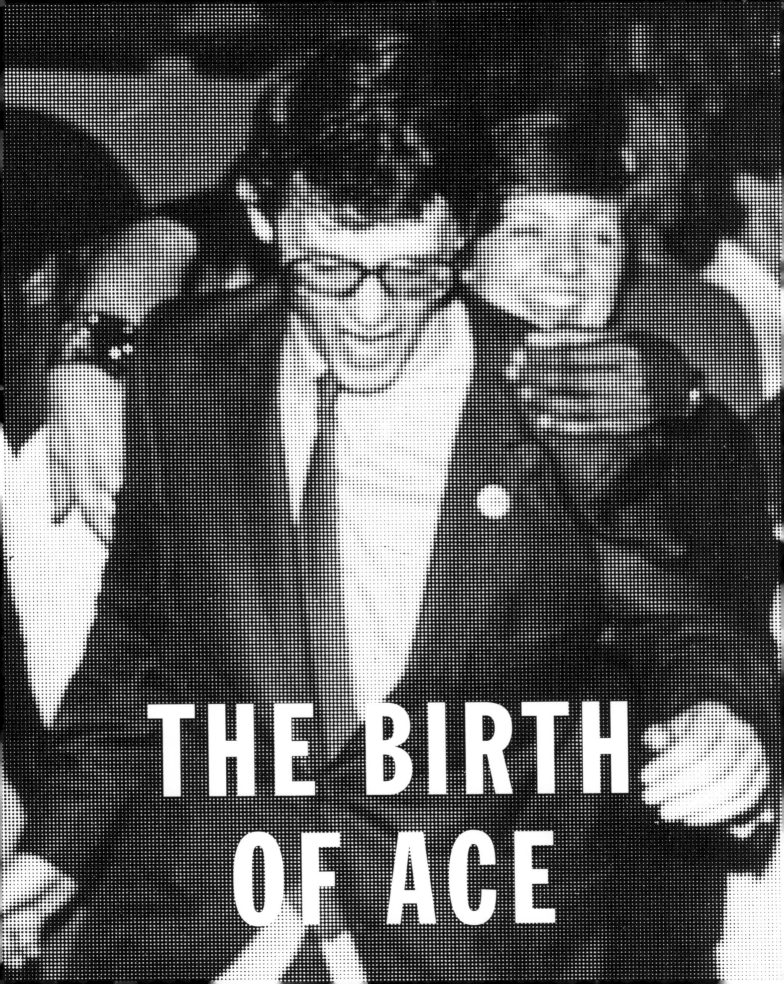

THE BIRTH OF ACE

THE BIRTH OF ACE

"I think one of the most fascinating things about Ace is the way in which it found a blueprint for being an independent label, beyond just acquiring hits", says Dean Rudland, one of the younger consultants for Ace Records:

> The normal blueprint is that you expand and you're bought out, or you grow and you explode. It's Factory versus Creation. There's no stage, as you expand, you need less money. If you have quite a big hit, then you need more money for a bigger hit. Put out six albums this year, you need to release eight albums the next. And very rapidly, you're making product, not records.

Chiswick's history was one of near misses, ill fortune and vulnerability in relation to the major labels when it came to trying to achieve hits. However, this might well have been a blessing in disguise. Chiswick's relative difficulty in securing a big act was, Roger Armstrong believes, the harbinger to their success, for it spawned Ace Records: "There was a big rockabilly/rock'n'roll scene that started in 1977. We were doing our stuff, Charly [Records] did theirs, MCA [Music Corporation of America] and RCA [Records] did retrospectives. So there was a reissue scene building." By 1978, Chiswick were already developing a reissue wing of their own. One of the earliest of these releases, was an album by Link Wray, whose pioneering, mean and fuzzy power chords set the tone for much of future 'white' rock'n'roll. They also set up a licensing deal with the American indie label Ace Records, which was based in Jackson, Mississippi. This was swiftly followed by the release of the single "Sea Cruise" by Frankie Ford and an album by Huey 'Piano' Smith.

The new reissue label needed a name and 'Ace' was chosen—partly in homage to the legendary British label Sue, which had also borrowed the name of another American-based indie label, and also because they felt that a name beginning with 'A' might give them an advantage when it came to being paid.

Part of the essential appeal of the earlier Ace label was its almost romantic failure. By failing to transmogrify into some huge, overweening corporation, it retained a reckless, heroic status as a rock label striving against the all the odds. And, when Chiswick originally approached EMI and failed to interest them in the reissue aspect of their label, their future success was sealed. As Armstrong recalls:

> All the while, in the late 1970s, while we were trying to make hits, we were putting out a steady stream of oldies, rock'n'roll and R&B. When we went to

OPPOSITE CLOCKWISE FROM TOP LEFT:
Hollywood Rock'n'Roll, the first Chiswick LP, with a classic cover shot from 1949; these cool cats were actually buying shirts on this pre-Photoshop mock up of the *Best of Ace Rockabilly*, 1981; *Ace Story: Vol 3*, circa 1990s; *Kings of Rockabilly*—the small but perfectly formed 10" album that was re-introduced by Ace; and Link Wray's *Early Recordings*, 1978, the sleeve of an iconic LP that introduced many to his grungy guitar sounds for the first time.

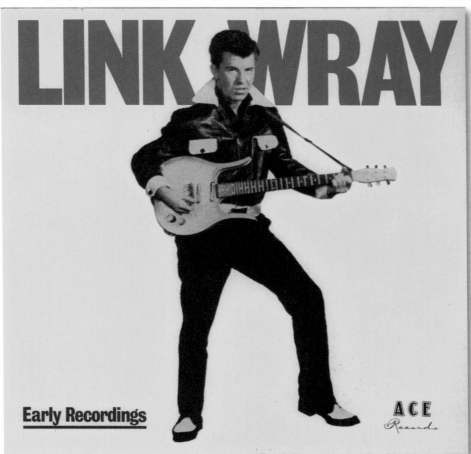

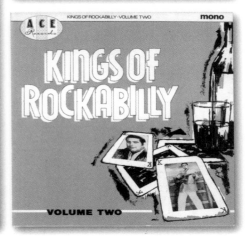

EMI it never dawned on us that they wouldn't want the whole package. They said they weren't interested in the reissues. So we moved that whole side of the operation onto Ace and put it out through Pinnacle, an independent distributor, who we are still with to this day. So that was all good, solid income—in those days you could sell 6,000–8,000 of a good blues compilation, partly because the market wasn't as crowded. So yes, it was a stroke of luck that EMI passed on our reissues…. By the early 1980s, Chiswick had gone, and we were Ace Records.

In 1979, Ace had embarked on a long-term programme of licensing deals with—and the eventually acquisition of—classic American labels that had fallen into neglect in their own country. There was a parallel here with the way in which acquiring that first batch of London records had helped kick-start the old market stall. This was the same thing, only on a much larger scale.

The first of these licensing deals were with Glad Music, in Houston, and Los Angeles-based Modern Records. After helping write sleeve notes for the Link Wray album, and some of the original Ace compilations, Ray Topping—a Rock On customer of long standing (and heavy duty record collector himself)— suggested that Ace contact Pappy Daily, director at Glad Music, to license some of his hillbilly and rockabilly masters. After a brief phone call with Daily, Ted Carroll flew out to Houston, returning just a few days later with a signed contract and the news that Daily had an office full of original master tapes by George Jones, rockabilly legend Sonny Fisher, Lightnin' Hopkins, Johnny & The Jammers (Johnny and Edgar Winter), Sleepy La Beef and many more. A month later, both he and Topping made a second trip to Houston and returned with enough tapes to compile half a dozen country and rockabilly albums. Later that year, again at Topping's suggestion, Ace contacted Modern Records in Los Angeles and secured a licensing deal that was to give the company permanent rights to a whole slew of seminal blues recordings by artists such as BB King, Elmore James, Howling Wolf, Ike Turner and Pee Wee Crayton.

Founded in 1945, by brothers Jules, Joe, Lester and Saul Bihari, Modern Records went on to launch several subsidiaries, including RPM, Flair, Meteor, and later, Kent. Modern were consistently one of the top-selling R&B companies in America. They issued the first recordings by Howling Wolf, as well as releases by Ike Turner (often credited as the originator of rock'n'roll after his production of "Rocket 88" by Jackie Brenston), John Lee Hooker and the great BB King, who said of Modern: "The company was never bigger than the artist. I could always talk to them." Today, the youngest and only surviving one of the brothers, Joe Bihari, continues to be active in music publishing. Bihari is still in touch

CLOCKWISE FROM TOP RIGHT:
Modern Records' catalogue, circa 1960s; Lightning Hopkins' "Jakehead Boogie", which features the first ever issue of the title track as it was recorded, 1999; and Ike Turner's *Rocks the Blues*, 1994, with a typical 'Fazio' cover from Crown Records.

OPPOSITE:
Early promotional shot of BB King, circa 1950s.

with many of the musicians and associates that were involved with Modern, and so remains an invaluable help to Ace.

By the 1960s, the music industry was changing. BB King had left Modern and signed with a rival, ABC Bluesway. Despite a continued presence in the R&B charts with releases from BB King, ZZ Hill, Ike and Tina Turner, The Ikettes and Little Richard on the Kent label, Modern Records was coming to depend mainly on its Crown budget label to maintain turnover.

By 1979, all that remained of the company was, in effect, its pressing plant— much of which was devoted to manufacturing poker chips rather than 33 rpms and 45 rpms. The recording studio now largely catered for Mexican acts. They did continue to sell a small proportion of their back catalogue, while many of the company's artists still lived locally (in the South Central area where the company was based). These included saxophonist, Joe Houston, who would occasionally visit the plant and, in lieu of royalties, walk out with boxes of his old albums.

The only one of the Bihari brothers still working with the label was Jules (although several of his sisters were now employed there too) and, when Carroll and Topping hooked up with him, they found him a man with whom it was difficult to do business. As they were making tape copies, he had the rather exasperating habit of ripping off the reel in mid-copy and running off with it. The vaults, meanwhile, had the sort of filing system that a small tornado would have done much to improve. However, with the dedicated patience of vinyl obsessives, Carroll and Topping trawled their way through the immense chaos and unearthed the long lost R&B treasures for which they were searching. By 1990, Ace acquired Modern Records and commenced with an inventory of the master tapes available, a process that continues to this day.

By 1981, Ace was beginning to build up a head of steam. They even started to release some contemporary recordings. These included American jump bluesmen, Roomful of Blues, but also British-based R&B bands such as Diz & The Doormen, Dana Gillespie and live favourites, Red Beans & Rice. Moreover, as the early 1980s kicked in, Ace found themselves at the leading edge of hipdom, with their releases featuring prominently in the pages of *NME*. This was not as unlikely as it first appeared and was strangely, but logically, connected with the punk/post-punk movement. For what the punk explosion had engendered was a new wave, not just of jerky young white bands in skinny ties, but also an emergent curiosity in rock'n'roll's origins and legends,

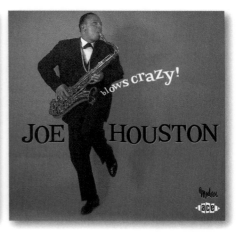

THAT DRIVING BEAT

RED BEANS & RICE

NEW SINGLE OUT MARCH 7th · CHISWICK RECORDS · CHIS 124

particularly in respect to soul and R&B. A classic route into this history might start with someone popular such as Elvis Costello. Costello had released his own version of Sam and Dave's "I Can't Stand up for Falling Down", just six months after buying a copy from Rock On. Devotees of the artist could work backwards, via Costello, finding themselves at the source. Journalists did the same thing. If all this smacked of a rather doubtful cult of authenticity concerning old soul music (which, by the mid-1980s led to a new breed of rather bland imitators such as Simply Red), by the early 1980s, it was a classic example of the refreshing 'shock of the old'. Such an interest was also a welcome boost for Ace's stock, and the mutual relationship was acknowledged when *NME* issued their free promotional Ace Case cassette in 1982.

ABOVE LEFT TO RIGHT:

Poster for Red Beans & Rice's "That Driving Beat", circa early 1980s. Image courtesy of the Undertakers. Cascade promotional poster.

"The great thing about Ace/Chiswick is that they were prepared to put out records that might only sell 1,000 copies each—but, of course, if you released enough of them the overall impact can be quite something", says Charlie Gillett. "Now, the storage space required to do this is quite formidable. In America, where land and property prices are cheaper, no one would bat an eyelid. But in Britain it presents quite a different problem." Indeed, with Ace now beginning to expand, doubling its output as each year passed, they were required to moved to newer, and more spacious premises, on Grafton Road in Kentish Town.

In addition to such expansion, and just as Chiswick was being wound down, Ace started up other labels. These included the budget imprint, Cascade, and most significantly, Kent Records (appropriated from the name of the subsidiary label at Modern) which would see the legendary northern soul aficionado 'Harboro Horace' (aka Ady Croasdell) enter the picture.

Croasdell started out as a general soul fan before drifting into northern soul: "The original mod clubs were all about people like Guy Stevens, the ones who had the best collection of import soul singles (he was obtaining them from whatever sources he had in London and playing them). You'd get a reputation as a soul DJ not so much for your personality as what you had in your box." Originally Croasdell was a collector who enjoyed the dancing and social aspect of the events but who, later, began dealing in records:

> In the early 1970s I worked on a stall in Rupert Street in Soho, in a barrow outside Cheapo Cheapo Records—here I learned that if I bought a record for 30p, I could sell it for 50p. The real price difference was in America. So eventually I took some of my records there, including my Jimmy Page stuff on Fontana, which were like gold dust over there, and bought up a load of rare northern soul records, selling them at Cleethorpes and Wigan Casino. Then, in 1979, Randy Cousins and I started up a soul club, the 6T'S, [originally at the Bedford Head, Maiden Lane, Covent Garden]) which is still running [at the 100 Club].

Croasdell was a fixture of the magical and mundane world of northern soul, which meant traversing England's dreary network of motorways and by-ways, to the Meccas and Casinos of Blackpool and Wigan, or down South to Berkhamsted, in search of northern soul all-day/all-night paradise. It was off the back of this success that Carroll invited Croasdell to compile an LP of tracks from the Kent/Modern catalogue. Having already stripped the catalogue of much of its rock'n'roll and R&B content, they realised there was a great deal of soul material available as well. The result, *For Dancers Only*, came out in 1982, and subsequently flew out of the shops. "By this time, it was the era of the mod revival and the new generation were looking for the authentic sounds that the original mods would have danced to—which had come into the northern soul domain—so there was a lot of crossover", recalls Croasdell.

There have been various crazes and fashions for old music that come and go, although usually leaving some kind of scene in their wake, be it swing, rockabilly, jazz-dance, two-step. However, from the Flamingo to the 100 Club's 6T'S dances, there was a continuous movement that never really ceased. Croasdell himself is always amazed at the longevity of the scene: "I never imagined it would last more than a few years. But it's endured a lot longer— there was a quirkiness about it that British collectors like. It was always there and kept picking up new fans all the time." And, as Peter Gibbon adds:

It's sometimes difficult for people to understand the depth of interest. When northern soul took off I wasn't in this country, I was in New York, so it was amazing for me to come back and see what was going on. Once, the soul singer, Barbara Lewis, came over to perform—and she had a number of songs that she'd been asked to sing—she stopped in one number and said to the audience: 'Whooah! How come you know the words to this song, and it's my song, and I can't remember the words myself?'

Lewis was one of many artists delighted to find that, forgotten in their own country, they were venerated in far-off European citadels like Cleethorpes —the sort of place of whose existence they had hitherto been sweetly and understandably oblivious. However, this simply typifies the paradox of the British-based northern soul scene, in which an audience from another time, another place and, for the large part, another race, grasp a music so firmly to their heart. It's an anomaly that often goes so unacknowledged as to make the relationship seem absolutely natural. Croasdell's highly entertaining sleeve notes to 6T'S Rhythm 'n' Soul Society: In the Beginning depict a bustling London underworld of pubs and clubs as parochially English as they come—Crackers, The Wheatsheaf and The Prince of Wales—populated with a dedicated fraternity of 'geezers' such as Cockney Mick, Barry, Taffy and his crew from Letchworth; a very modish scene of faces, snappy suits, haircuts and old school moves. There is both a disconnection yet, at the same time, an extraordinarily strong connection, between the people consuming the music in the present day and the people who made it—Carolyn Crawford, Lowell Fulson, The Temptations, Danny White, to name a few. Rock music has been described a "fascination with America", often entailing the embarrassing spectacle of rock fans affecting black American mannerisms in modes of dress and speech. There is little sign of this in the northern soul scene; rather, an unabashed, almost ribald Britishness (although, a sense of purism and disdain for those whose knowledge of such music begins and ends at Motown and Stax Records, does often prevail). "The 1960s was a renaissance period, there was such an explosion of activity all over black America—B-sides, records that hardly sold

ABOVE LEFT TO RIGHT:
For Dancers Only, the first ever Kent LP, 1982, and Tony Middleton, Brad Comer, Ady Croasdell, Mary Love, circa 1991.

OPPOSITE CLOCKWISE FROM TOP LEFT:
100 Club flyer from 1982; *6T's Rhythm 'n' Soul Society*, commemorating the 25th anniversary of the 6T's Club, 2004; poster for an event at 6T's, commemorating its seventh anniversary, 1986; Mary Love's "Hey Stoney Face"—the first 6T's anniversary 45, 1984; and a membership card for 6T's, illustrated with a picture of the Marvelettes.

any, little ghetto labels, then master tapes, acetates, things that never came out because they were producing so much stuff", says Croasdell:

> As ever, it wasn't the stuff that made the charts that was the best. There were chart toppers that were atrocious and records that sold ten copies that are absolute bloody masterpieces. It's a very critical scene, in which things are appreciated purely on artistic merit…. The northern soul scene can be a bit up its arse, in that it claims the music as its own, when it isn't really its own at all, it's the music of black America.

The *For Dancers Only* series proved hugely successful and spread beyond the haunts and cellars of the British northern soul scene. Says Croasdell: "There was nobody else doing the same sort of thing, and we did it with a considerable amount of style. The place where it had real impact was in Europe—France, Italy, Germany, Spain—where young mods had never had anything like a northern soul scene. Kent had that mystical function that Motown had held for British kids in the 1960s." The irony of a mod scene developing in Italy—Italian kids feeding off a British-born scene which aped Italian styles—is enough to make any cultural commentator's head swim.

In recent years, the northern soul scene has spread to, of all places, North America. "People in America had no idea as to what northern soul was until about ten years ago—but then, all of a sudden, everyone wanted top dollar for these things", says Croasdell. "I get American kids come over to my weekender at Cleethorpes who got into the scene via Kent [Records]."

Croasdell's only concern is that, despite the timelessness of northern soul and the still-undiscovered treasures of soul in general, the twenty-first century may see the genre transform into: "A dinosaur-collecting scene, an oldies scene—like the rockabilly thing—about people trying to preserve lost youth. A lot of it is historical documentation and has become quite academic over the past few years. I even gave a talk at the V&A on northern soul music in the old lecture theatre that's been there since the 1850s."

That said, the rediscovery of northern soul is always just around the corner. There was a big revival in the wake of britpop in the mid-1990s and, while the scene could hardly be described as in 'upswing' now, there remain websites, occasional club nights and events dedicated to its preservation, as well as, of course, the perennial 6T'S.

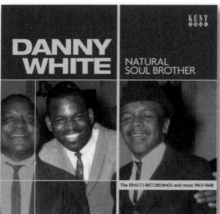

KENT

R E C O R D S

132-134, Grafton Road, Kentish Town, London, N.W.5

VARIOUS ARTISTS - ON THE SOUL SIDE KENT 006

16 TRACKS ON WAX THAT CUT A SOLID SOUL
GROOVE STRAIGHT TO YOUR HEART. FROM THE
GOLDEN ERA OF SOUL, KENT RECORDS PRESENTS
ONE OF THE MOST DYNAMIC COMPILATIONS TO HIT
YOUR RECORD DECK IN YEARS. FROM THE OPENING
STRAINS OF PATRICE HOLLOWAY'S LOVE & DESIRE
RIGHT THROUGH TO THE HURT OF TIMI YURO'S
"WHAT'S A MATTER BABY" THERE IS SATISFACTION
GUARANTEED ON EVERY CUT. "ON THE SOUL SIDE" IS
DRAWN FROM THE VAULTS OF THE CAPITOL &
LIBERTY LABELS AND IS A HARBORO HORACE
COMPILATION IN THE TRADITION OF KENT'S
EARLIER RELEASES, "FOR DANCERS ONLY", "FOR
DANCERS ALSO" AND "SLOW'N'MOODY, BLACK AND
BLUESY"

SOUL

G R O O V E S

CLOCKWSIE FROM TOP LEFT:
The first Town 45, designed by Vicki Fox for Jackie Wilson's "I Don't Want to Lose You", 1985; advertisement for Kent Records, 1983; and Maxine Brown's *It's Torture*, 1985, one of the biggest northern soul finds from the Kent archeologists.

OPPOSITE:
Dave Hamilton, circa 1970s. Hamilton owned a number of labels but was also a regular player and writer with Motown.

One tremendous offshoot of northern soul's revivalism is, of course, the positive effect it can have on the lives of the artists themselves. Croasdell takes up the story of Ann Bridgeforth (aka Little Ann), a singer whose early career consisted of one single, on a label run by Dave Hamilton (a Detroit soul producer kicked out of Motown for attempting to unionise the label's house band, the brilliant Funk Brothers, of whom he was a member):

> We ended up buying all the tapes from Dave Hamilton's widow after he died. We knew there was one gem in there—Richard Searling, a northern soul DJ, had been playing an acetate called "When He's Not Around" and no one knew who it was by exactly. Then we realised it was one of Hamilton's unissued Little Ann recordings. And we found a whole lot more, as well as "Who Are You Trying To Fool", which has been called the greatest 'non-Motown' Motown record ever made. Eventually, she had four or five tracks released which became so well-known that she went from working in a Chrysler stockroom in Detroit to singing in front of a 1,000 people in the Cleethorpes ballroom, and pretty stunned by the fact that her records had come out at all.

Perhaps the last word should go to Armstrong, speaking in 1983 to Dave Henderson from *Sounds*. He predicted:

> It's not just a breed of purists who are buying the Kent albums, the music seems to reach much further than that. Most people seem to be going back and looking at older music and it's that new generation of kids who are doing that, who are going to be making the next great important music. They'll be influenced by everything from rock'n'roll to northern soul and back again. There's never anything new in music, it's just the way that people compile things into a sound. It will be very interesting to see what gets thrown up from it all.

WHIRLWIND GIG POSTER, CIRCA 1970S.

Whirlwind played for five days at this regular event (which also included live music by various rock'n'roll DJs and a number of dance competitions) held at the Notre Dame Hall in London. Whirlwind was founded by Nigel Dixon (vocals) and Phil Hardy (drums), and also consisted of band members Mick Lewis (guitar) and Chris Emo (bassist).

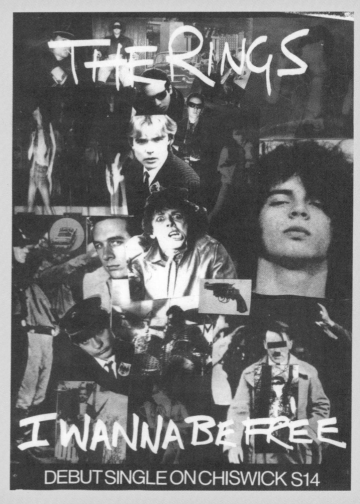

WHIRLWIND GIG POSTER, CIRCA 1970S.

THE RINGS PROMOTIONAL POSTER, 1977.

Whirlwind released two albums with the Chiswick label, *Blowing Up a Storm* and *In The Studio*. *Blowing Up a Storm*, 1978, was the band's debut album (the cover of which was designed by Barney Bubbles). After the success of their second album *Midnight Blue*, they were due to tour with Blondie, but this fell through when band member, Gerry Hassett, fell ill.

"I Wanna Be Free" was the only release by The Rings to be featured on Chiswick's *The Chiswick Story*. The Rings were formed by John Alder (aka Twink) who had previously played with such psychedelic outfits as Tomorrow and The Pink Fairies. The band regularly played at the 100 Club and Roxy.

SEA CRUISE PROMOTIONS' ROCKIN RIVERBOAT HOP POSTER, 1982.

Ace band, Diz & The Doormen, belted out their characteristic British R&B at this one off, and rather eclectic, event on an the Elizabethan riverboat. The group were accompanied by Dynamite Band who released the (now very rare) *Rockin' Is Our Business* on Chiswick.

ACE RECORDS TENTH ANNIVERSARY POSTER, 1985.

The usual suspects are featured on this colourful poster celebrating the label's tenth anniversary—Motorhead, BB King, The Cramps, Little Richard, 3 Mustaphas 3, to name but a few.

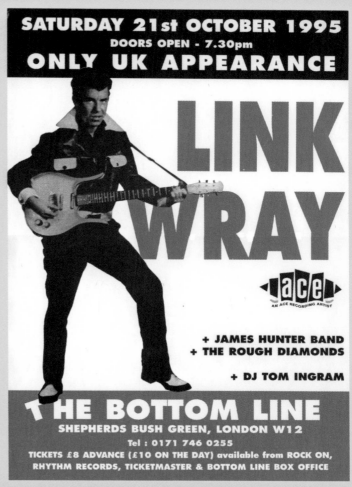

OPPOSITE: THE TABLE'S "SEX CELLS" PROMOTIONAL POSTER, 1978.

The Table originally hailed from Cardiff, Wales, and it was this single for which they were best known. The band was comprised by Russell Young (vocals), Tony Barnes (guitar and bass), Len Lewis (drums) and Micky O'Connor (guitar). "Sex Cells" was one of only of a handful of releases by the band—the most successful being "Do The Standing Still", 1977. Another of their singles "The Magical Melon of the Tropics" was championed by NME as "a seething turmoil of furious punk rhythms, multitracked psychedlic guitars and bizarre comic book lyrics"—a response, perhaps, to their ability to transcend and combine musical genres.

LEFT: BEAT GOES PUBLIC PROMOTIONAL POSTER, CIRCA 1980S.

This poster features the first four albums released by the label: *Mongo Santamaria*, *Do It Fluid: Six Rare Grooves*, *Cal Tjader* and *Focus on Fusion*.

RIGHT: POSTER FOR LINK WRAY'S THE BOTTOM LINE GIG, 1995.

The Bottom Line was an event regularly held at Shepherds Bush Empire that showcased some of the most talented rock, pop and country artists of the day. This event would have been one of the last Link Wray played in Britain, as he passed away in 2005.

ACE RECORDS' TWENTIETH ANNIVERSARY POSTER, 1995.

This poster highlights the incredible range and diversity of the label, and its artists, in a period spanning just 20 years.

ACE RECORDS PROMOTIONAL FLYER, CIRCA 1980S.

The flyer lists just a small selection of the outstanding collection of blues music on the Ace label. Among the celebrated albums are *The Ace Story* (volumes one and two), *Ike Turner and His Kings of Rhythm: Vol 1*, *The Best of BB King* and *Teenage Rock'n'Roll Party*.

OPPOSITE: TAKOMA RECORDS PROMOTIONAL POSTER FEATURING JOHN FAHEY, LEO KOTTKE AND ROBBIE BASHO, CIRCA 1980S.

Fahey, Kottke and Basho are all upheld as pioneers of the acoustic guitar. All three are associated with the American Primitivism Movement (also known as American Primitive Guitar), which champions avant-garde compositions using traditional country blues finger picking techniques.

3 Mustaphas 3 had great success with this album, as well as the three others they released on the GlobeStyle label; *Soup of The Century*, *Shopping* and *Heart of Uncle*.

OPPOSITE: THE CRAMPS TOUR POSTER, 1991.

This poster reflects the anarchy so typical of the band. The Town and Country Club was a regular host to pyschedlic/garage bands such as The Cramps and also the venue where Kent Records held it's twenty-fifth anniversary. It is now better known as the London Forum, after being renamed by *Mean Fiddler* when they bought the venue in 1993.

ALBANIA PROMOTIONAL PAMPHLET, FOR "ARE YOU ALL MINE", CIRCA 1980S.

"Are You All Mine" was one of the 16 singles featured on the album *Life After Death Is On The Phone*. The band moved from Glasgow to London in 1978 and, after a session in a recording studio in the Clyde Estuary, released this Big Beat album, which contains some of their finest works.

THE CRAMPS

LONDON TOUR SUPPORTS – 1991 TOUR
TOWN & COUNTRY CLUB, LONDON NW5

DOORS OPEN 7.00pm ALL NIGHTS ● CRAMPS ON STAGE 9.30pm ALL NIGHTS EXCEPT FRIDAY – 9.00pm ● ALL SHOWS END 11.00pm EXCEPT FRIDAY – 10.30pm
TICKETS £8.50 ADVANCE ● T.C. BOX OFFICE 071 284 0303 ● T.C. CREDIT CARD STATION 071 284 1221 ● & ROCK ON / ROUGH TRADE

FRIDAY OCTOBER 25th
SAVAGE FAITH
ON STAGE 7.20 – 7.40pm
THE GOLDEN HORDE
ON STAGE 8.00 – 8.30pm

TUESDAY OCTOBER 29th
THE CANNIBALS
ON STAGE 7.30 – 8.00pm
THE PHANTOM CHORDS
ON STAGE 8.15 – 9.00pm

SATURDAY OCTOBER 26th
THEE HEADCOATS
Steamdriven! ON STAGE 7.30 – 8.00pm
THE GOLDEN HORDE
ON STAGE 8.15 – 9.00pm

WEDNESDAY OCTOBER 30th
THE EARLS OF SUAVE
ON STAGE 7.30 – 8.00pm
RONNIE DAWSON
ON STAGE 8.15 – 9.00pm

Scala CLUB CINEMA
275-277 PENTONVILLE ROAD, LONDON N1

SUNDAY OCTOBER 27th
HORROR PARTY BEACH 5.05 9.30
FRANKENSTEIN MEETS
THE SPACE MONSTER 3.35 8.00
A BUCKET OF BLOOD 2.10 6.35
TRASH TRIPLE BILL FOR CRAMPS DAY OFF

THURSDAY OCTOBER 31st
THE JOHNSON FAMILY
ON STAGE 7.30 – 8.00pm
GALLON DRUNK
ON STAGE 8.15 – 9.00pm

Design : Technimedia □ Print : I.P.S.

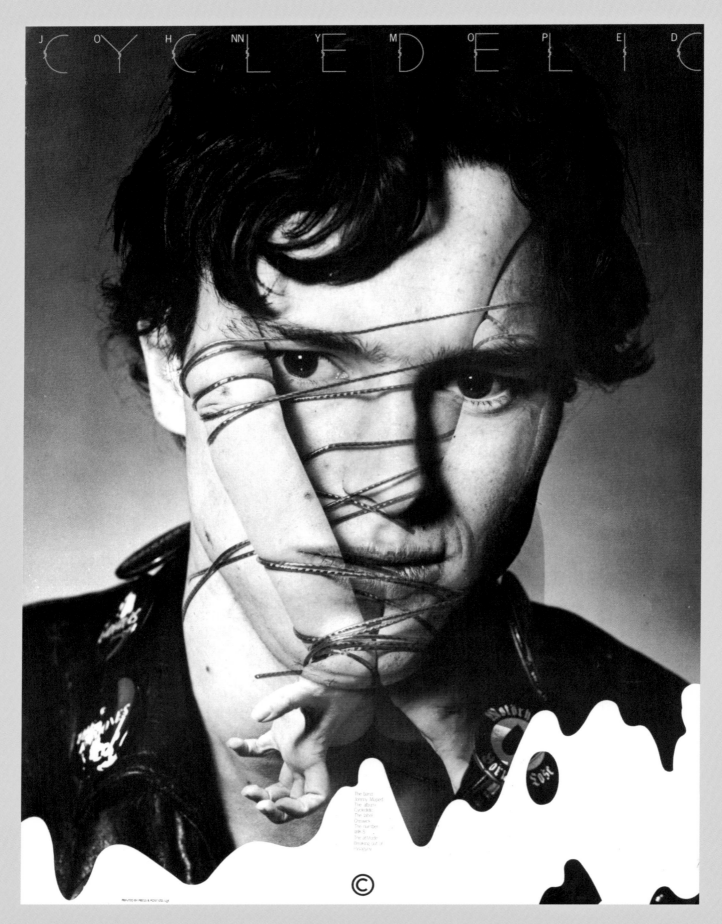

JOHNNY MOPED CLUB FLYER, CIRCA 1970S.

This flyer served as admission to the renowned jazz club, Ronnie Scotts, in London. Usually catering to a jazz crowd, Johnny Moped's punk rock delivery might have come as somewhat as a shock to the club's typical audience. Moped, however, was not completely oblivious to the genre—having previously played with a number of jazz musicians, including guitarist, Alan Holdsworth, for example.

OPPOSITE: JOHNNY MOPED PROMOTIONAL POSTER FOR CYCLEDELIC ON CHISWICK RECORDS, CIRCA 1970S.

Cycledelic, which was released on Chiswick in 1978, featured backing vocals from Captain Sensible as one of the Mopettes. In previous incarnations, band members also included Chrissie Hynde and Slimey Toad. Along the bottom of this poster the fine print reads:
The band: Johnny Moped
The album: *Cycledelic*
The Attitude: Breaking out of misogyny

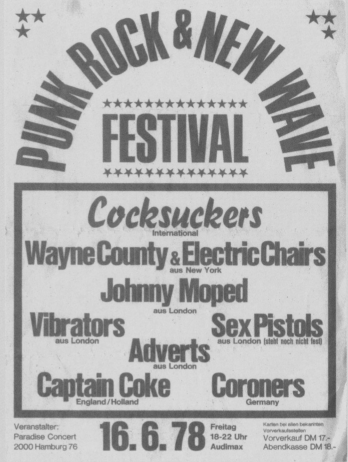

PUNK ROCK AND NEW WAVE FESTIVAL POSTER, HAMBURG, GERMANY, 1978.

This poster features Chiswick regular, Johnny Moped. While this Hamburg show was cancelled, the likelihood of Moped turning up was never certain anyway. He was renowned for his reluctance to take part in studio sessions and is famed, on one particular occasion, for being found by his band members queuing for the very gig at which he was meant to be performing.

LITTLE BOB STORY PROMOTIONAL STICKER, CIRCA 1970S.

Little Bob Story has a number of releases included in Chiswick's *The Chiswick Story* and *Submarine Tracks & Fools Gold: Chiswick Chartbusters* albums. French-born front man, Roberto Piazza (aka Little Bob), joined forces with Gremy Guy-Georges (guitar), Backbeard (bass) and Mino Quertier (drums), in 1974, to form the group. A rock band inspired by French blues, Little Bob Story released such songs as "Do Not Let Me Be Misunderstood", 1975, and the album *High Time*, in 1976.

CHISWICK POSTER FOR LITTLE BOB STORY'S OFF THE RAILS, CIRCA 1970S.

Off the Rails was the LP that superceded the very successful *High Time* album. Produced in England by Sean Tyla, it includes such classics as "Don't Let Me Be Misunderstood" and "Tobacco Road".

BIG BEAT

BIG BEAT

Big Beat Records was set up in 1980 because Ted Carroll thought that Johnny & The Jammers' 45 was a tad too 1960s-oriented for release on Ace, and might damage the 1950s style credibility of the parent label. The first significant release on the former label was Motorhead's *Beerdrinkers and Hell Raisers* EP. (The four tracks on this release had been recorded back in 1977, but not included on the original *Motorhead* LP.)

The Chiswick label, including the *Motorhead* album, was licensed to EMI for Britain until 1981. At the suggestion of Motorhead's manager, Doug Smith, it was decided to release the remaining four titles on an EP. *Beerdrinkers and Hell*

LEFT TO RIGHT:

Rockabilly Psychosis, 1984—a landmark release in the history of manic rock'n'roll, and Johnny & The Jammers "School Day Blues"—the first Big Beat 45 and reissue of early Johnny Winter outing, circa 1980s.

OPPOSITE:

Big Beat poster featuring a rare picture of Nigel Dixon from Whirlwind with ex-101er, Joe Strummer, circa 1980s.

Raisers, which came in 7" and 12" formats, as well as a variety of tasteful shades of coloured vinyl, was released on Big Beat Records rather than Chiswick, so that the money earned could flow directly into the company's needy coffers, rather than be swallowed up in recouping Chiswick advances from EMI. This proved to be a shrewd move as it made it into the Top 40, shifting over 40,000 units in the process.

Big Beat became, among other things, a nursery label for Chiswick. It was also home to the sort of material EMI would not have been interested in when dealing with Chiswick—low budget, scuzzy, furry, oddball garage rock, assorted mutations of R&B and rock'n'roll—particularly of the sort that encrusted the underbelly of 1960s pop (music that was never going to chart but nonetheless deserved a home).

Such a band were The Meteors, one of the first British rockabilly groups to take on board the principles of The Cramps; in creating a viable British version of psychobilly, which mixed punk sensibility, rockabilly and a lurid, horror comic book take on early rock'n'roll. They had formed in 1980 but found themselves shunned by traditional rockabilly types, or the "old dinosaurs" as P Paul Fenech, their vocalist/guitarist, put it.

"The second show we did, one of the teddy boys came up, pulled out all the plugs and said, 'You can't play rockabilly, your drummer's got green hair!'", remembers The Meteors then manager, Nick Garrard. "So we got paid and asked to leave. But Sonny Burgess, who made some of the best records for Sun Records in the 1950s, he dyed his hair green. And pink. Does that mean he couldn't make rockabilly?"

As Carroll recalls: "Towards the end of 1980, Nick Garrard approached Chiswick to see if we would be interested in releasing the soundtrack to a short movie being made by some friends of his, which was to feature the band as well as comedian Keith Allen". And so the *Meteor Madness* EP came into being and was initially issued on Ace, rather than Big Beat, at Garrard's insistence, although later re-pressings were issued on the latter.

The Meteors second single "Radioactive Kid" was first released by Big Beat before transferring to EMI-distributed Chiswick. So also was The Textones' "I Can't Fight It" which, after picking up airplay on Big Beat, was quickly transferred to Chiswick. The B-side of The Textones 45—"Vacation" written by bassist Kathy Valentine—reached new heights of success when her new band, The Go Go's, had an immense hit with the song.

"The Meteors were very good but it was The Stray Cats, The Jets, who got big, The Meteors were too on the edge, really, they were a punky version of rockabilly with attitude", says Roger Armstrong. Then there was Billy Childish, musician, poet, novelist, painter and associate of the artist, Tracey Emin, who had featured prominently in her famous tent piece. "We seemed to get involved with people who would become very influential later on. The Milkshakes and Billy were a massive influence on the Seattle scene", remembers Armstrong:

BELOW LEFT TO RIGHT:
Milkshakes promotional card, and an American trade magazine advertisement for one of the four LPs released by the Milkshakes.

OPPOSITE:
Outsider Art poster for The Guana Batz, circa mid-1980s. Image courtesy of Roger Armstrong.

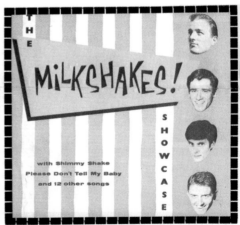

 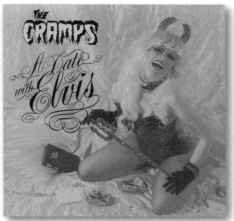 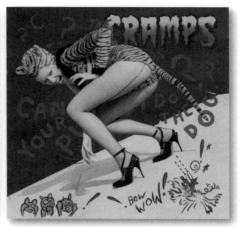

But then, what we've done as a label has always been rooted in DIY and the kind of individuality that we saw in rock'n'roll, more than the constructed approach of, say, more pompous forms of music. And that's what we saw in the garage bands of the mid-1980s—by which time our whole reissues project was really rolling and neither the bands or ourselves were under any illusions about getting hit singles any more.

The first two 45s by The Meteors helped inspire a legion of bands with strange haircuts, and often stranger names, to take up drums, guitar and string bass, and venture forth into the world of psychobilly (or, at least, variations of this genre). Soon, a myriad of such bands were beating a path to Ace's door—among them; The Guana Batz, The Poorboys, Restless, The Vibes and The Geezers. Another example of the type of group Big Beat worked with was The Stingrays. As Alec Palao, the American-based English expat, one time member of the band and subsequent Ace consultant, recalls: "The band was an amalgam of everything we were into, be it rockabilly, garage punk, 1970s punk, surf, northern soul, folk-rock; we were omnivores." The Stingrays were the classic example of a band who had supersized on Ace's ever-increasing and eclectic output of lost music.

However, Big Beat's biggest catch was The Cramps. "I connected with them through an old friend, Steve Pross, from the market stall days whose father worked at Pan Am. He got very cheap flights to and from America, so was able to trade records across the Atlantic", recalls Armstrong:

> He then went to work for Enigma Records and approached me, saying they had The Cramps' *Smell of Female* album, but had no representation in Europe, and did we want to do it. We jumped at it. It all peaked around the *A Date With Elvis* LP. That was an amazing time. They played The Hammersmith Palais three nights running, toured Europe and then came back and played the Hammersmith Odeon twice.

Certainly, The Cramps were a far larger proposition than Ace had been used to for quite some time. Suddenly, they found themselves up to their neck in work, with records to ship, journalists with whom to liaise and tours to co-arrange. Having formed as early as 1972 in California (around the nucleus of Lux Interior and Poison Ivy), The Cramps were initially located on the fringes of the Country, Blue Grass and Blues Club's punk scene. However, their abiding, almost necrophilic, love of early rock'n'roll quickly prompted their

OPPOSITE:
The Stingrays pose with Ace consultant, Alec Palao (bottom right), circa 1980s.

ABOVE LEFT TO RIGHT:
Big Beat compilation, *These Cats Ain't Nothin' But Trash*, featuring The Stingrays, Milkshakes and The Cannibals, 1983; The Cramps' *A Date With Elvis*, 1986; and the original artwork for The Cramps' "Can Your Pussy do the Dog?", 1985. Image courtesy of Lux Interior.

mutation into the first psychobilly group. They were as much influenced by the rawhide guitar sounds of Link Wray as they were The Ramones. They progressed, with songs such as "Human Fly" and "Goo Goo Muck", comprised by rock'n'roll sounds, sci-fi horror, B-movie pulp and lost Americana. It was front man, Lux Interior's belief, that rock'n'roll had represented a cathartic moment that would prove transcendent for all mankind, but all that was left was a sense of mourning for what had passed. Of course, The Cramps were a mutant amalgam of elements undreamt of in the 1950s—the sort of group who could only have existed with the benefit of hindsight—a very 1980s group, in other words, and justly lauded both by critics and the emergent British Goth audience who worshipped them. After the live recording of *Smell of Female* (issued in 1983), which included the typically Elvis-twisted single "You Ain't Nothing but a Gorehound", came "A Date With Elvis"—dedicated with typical

ABOVE:
Poison Ivy posing on the cover of The Cramps' 1991 tour programme. Image courtesy of Roger Armstrong.

OPPOSITE:
Big Beat advertisement featured in The Cramps' 1991 tour programme. Image courtesy of Roger Armstrong.

black humour, but real sincerity, to Ricky Nelson; the teen idol destined to die young in a plane crash in 1985.

"The Cramps were a great band, still are to this day", says Armstrong. In truth, The Cramps represented a high point for Big Beat which, over the years, gradually diminished as the indie scene took a further downshift. Says consultant, Dean Rudland:

> Sometime around the mid-1980s, Britain lost its ability to sustain indie bands of a certain size. I remember groups like The Prisoners, they'd tour, they'd happily sell 5,000 or 6,000 copies of their albums, they'd get nowhere near having a hit, nor were they trying to. They were an indie band, no doubt about it, they weren't in that chart world. At some time just past that period, the industry stopped being able to support bands in that way. You were either a big success, or you were nothing.

As a consequence, in its later years, Big Beat has concentrated on expanding its back catalogue, which is now a veritable index of sublimely scuzzy rock'n'roll eccentricity, with Palao—now based near San Francisco—involved in compiling CDs, researching owners of the tapes and finding bands to interview for his sleeve notes. And so, Big Beat have been responsible for disinterring albums by The Chocolate Watch Band, The Music Machine and Strawberry Alarm Clock, all of whom are fondly name-checked in interviews by Rock's more sonically ambitious young turks, as well as The Fugs and The Zombies, whose *Odessey and Oracle* (sic) represents—to those who have heard it—a whole 1960s as yet unspoiled by constant radio play and nostalgia fests.

Palao really developed Big Beat's 1960s catalogue with the *Nuggets from the Golden State* series, the ultimate in West Coast archaeology. In America, he

ABOVE LEFT TO RIGHT:
Zombies souvenir programme for the launch of the box set Zombie Heaven, 1997 at the Jazz Café (within hours they were selling for £100 on eBay), and The Zombies promotional shot, 1968.

OPPOSITE CLOCKWISE FROM TOP:
The Zombies' *Odessey and Oracle* (original CBS sleeve), 1968; The Strawberry Alarm Clock's *The Strawberry Alarm Clock*, 1992; The Music Machine's *The Ultimate Turn On*, 2006; Chocolate Watchband's *Melts in Your Brain… Not on Your Wrist*, 2005; and The Nuggets' *The Hush Records Story*, one of the releases from The Golden State series, 1997.

gained unlimited access to the old producers and to the artists, and even played bass in The Chocolate Watch Band. Against all odds, he has managed to obtain the agreement of the members of the legendary gun-toting The Charlatans to finally release their early demos—eliciting an entire CD from a band who had previously issued only one 45 at the time. But it wasn't just West Coast bands that had Palao enthralled. More than any, The Zombies were his holy grail. After the opportunity arose to work on their catalogue, Palao compiled a four CD box set within hours. Rightly lauded as one of the best box sets ever, it cemented The Zombies' position as one of the finest British bands of the mid-1960s, despite only having two proper hits. Palao's research and Phil Smee's design were comensurated by Carol Fawcett into a luxurious package that has been one of Ace's biggest sellers.

Palao now spends much of his time as Ace's 'tape rat', travelling all over America armed with a mini studio. Along the way, he has cut deals that have produced a huge amount of catalogue material in order to feed the hungry Ace machine. In 1993, he recompiled The Sonics' releases into another, hugely successful, CD. In 2004, their version of "Have Love Will Travel" became the soundtrack for, of all things, the Land Rover advert. These rights create very large and valuable income for the company, allowing it the occasional indulgence in the worthy, but not necessarily economically-sound, release.

ABOVE LEFT TO RIGHT:
The Prisoners' *Electric Fit*, 1984; The Sonics' *Boom* (original Etiquette sleeve), 1966; and The Sonics "Here Are The Sonics!!!" (original Etiquette sleeve), 1965. Images courtesy of Jim Lahat.

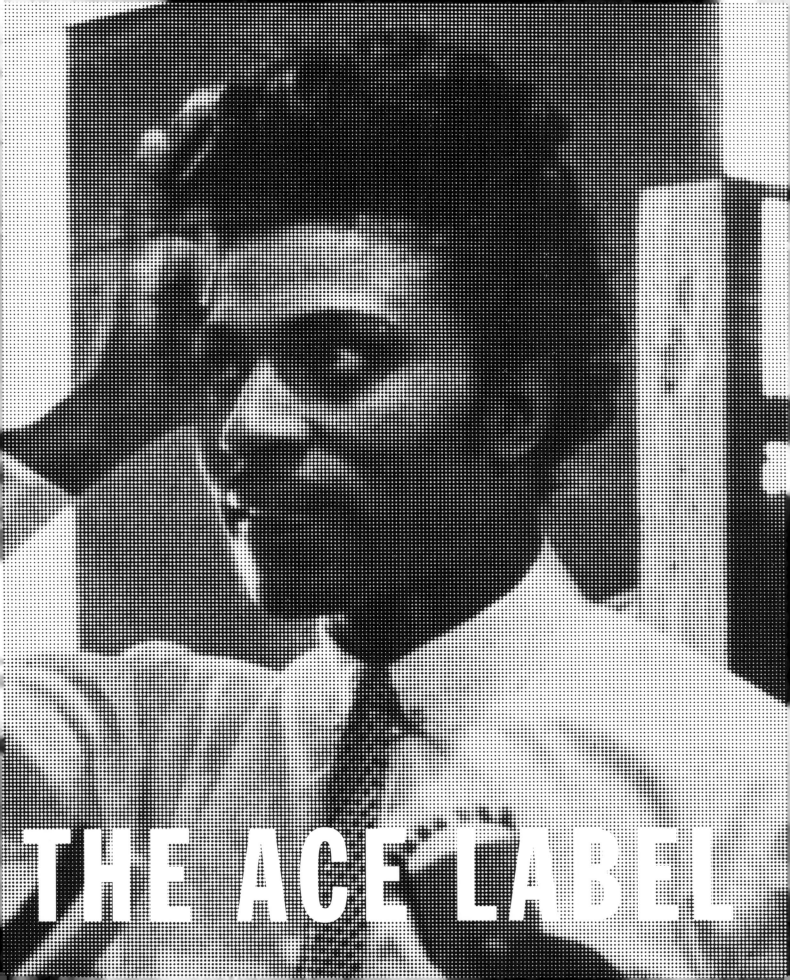

THE ACE LABEL

At the same time as Kent was inaugurated, Ace licensed Cadence Records, with albums by the Everly Brothers, Johnny Tillotson and The Chordettes (a copy of whose 1983 Ace-designed album sleeve crops up in one of the opening scenes of the film, *Back to the Future*—a tribute to Ace's ability to produce an authentic look).

In 1983, Ted Carroll brought over a caravan of American 1950s R&B stars; Willie Egan, Chuck Higgins, Young Jessie and Big Jay McNeely, all of who played Camden's Electric Ballroom in August of the same year. Carroll and Ray Topping had met the musicians while in Los Angeles, excavating more tape and acetate masters from the Modern Records vaults, and discovered that they were interested doing a show London.

Big Jay McNeeley is just one example of the prodigious talent Ace exists to showcase. A formidable 'honking' saxophonist, he was also known for his onstage aerobatics, which saw him banned from many venues in his native Los Angeles—such was the excitement they provoked among the city's emergent teen scene. He retired from music in the 1970s and became a mailman but, by 1983, he started touring again, with Carroll's revue one of the important fixtures in the event of his return. Even in 1999, aged 72, he was raising hell at the Apollo Theatre, jumping into the audience and playing a fluorescent saxophone while break dancing.

In 1984, their output ever-expanding, Ace were forced to move to Steele Road in Harlesden (where they still continue to reside). Their output of reissues ran the gamut from R&B and doo-wop to 1950s novelty pop and twangy rock'n'roll. And yet, when it came to technology, Ace were then—as now—state of the art. Although CD production was still some way down the timeline, this was the year in which Ace discovered digital tape recorders—in the guise of the Sony Betamax/SLF1 system—acquired for a very reasonable £1,500 by their post-production engineer, Adam Skeaping. Not only would this allow Ace to make perfect copies of analogue tapes, but they saved a fortune on tape, as the system used two-hour Betamax cassettes costing one tenth of the analogue tape stock.

1984 also saw Ace acquire the licence to Laurie Records and, as a result, the rights to their tapes. Laurie's tape librarian, Bruce Hailstock, was only too happy to hand over to Roger Armstrong. "I've been tripping over them for the last 20 years", Hailstock told him. One of the first discoveries Armstrong made,

OPPOSITE CLOCKWISE FROM TOP LEFT:
The Chordettes LP sleeve, which was designed by Ace and features in the film *Back To The Future*, alongside period 1950s albums; (Left to right) John Crosby, Gail Clark, Yvette De Roy, Phil Stoker, Mike Beard and Chris Popham; Ace advertisement for the Everly Brothers in mono sound, circa 1980s; Original Johnny Tillotson billboard advertisement, 1965; and *The Laurie Records Story: Vol 1*, 2003.

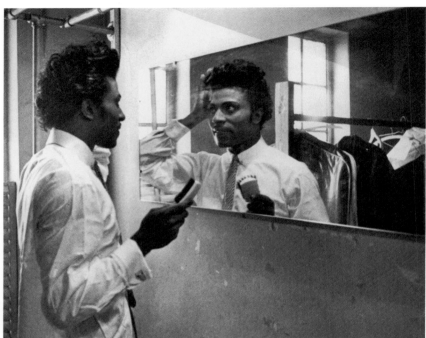

was of the original masters of the Dion & The Belmonts sessions in the late 1950s, including unissued material that had previously been thought not to exist.

Dion & The Belmonts were typical of the vocal groups that seemed to spring up on every street corner during the rock'n'roll era, many having evolved from street gangs. Their name was even appropriated from a local avenue. After a few false starts, they landed up on Laurie Records and immediately had a hit with "I Wonder Why", a single that resounded through every city neighbourhood, from open windows and car doors, radios and record players. "Every kid did his five-and-dime imitation of Carlo [Mastrangelo's] staccato bass intro, and that became one of the signature sounds of the rock'n'roll age", wrote JC Marion (a contemporary of the group) in *Doo-wop Nation* magazine: "Dion & The Belmonts came off the starting line in full stride and never looked back." They enjoyed a series of hits, quite often with maudlin tales of unrequited, or unfulfilled, teenage love and managed to survive Dion DiMucci's departure well into the 1960s before shifts in trends finally saw their demise.

For years, fans of the group had to put up with poorly dubbed tapes, often marred by their transformation into reprocessed fake stereo. Now, Armstrong was able to take the original master tapes to Associated Studios (in itself a legend, as many of the Brill Building demos were cut there) and at last make impeccable copies of them. Their clarity, even on vinyl, was lauded by the critics. However, there was more in store for Ace. 1984 was also the year in which they secured a long-term deal with Art Rupe's Specialty Records, thereby acquiring a crack at Little Richard's back catalogue. Rupe was born Arthur Goldberg in 1917, and started Speciality Records immediately after the Second World War having determined—by a quasi-scientific process—the exact formula required to make a 'race' record commercially successful (one that cleverly mixed gospel and secular passions). Although he kept an extremely low profile within the music business, he had a high hit rate. Among his earliest successes were Sister Wynona Carr and Roy Milton. However, it was with Little Richard that Rupe

ABOVE LEFT TO RIGHT:
Dion DiMucci in the studio, circa 1950s. Image courtesy of Dion DiMucci. Little Richard attends to his process in his dressing room, circa 1950s. Image courtesy of Specialty Records, Concord Music Group, Inc.

OPPOSITE:
Original Little Richard billboard advertisement for his 1964 comeback (in the guise of the 45 "Bama Lama Loo") on Specialty Records.

LITTLE RICHARD _RETURNS_

To *POP* Recording...

And He Has A *HIT!*

"BAMA LAMA BAMA LOO"

by

Little RICHARD

★

Specialty #692

Specialty Records
8300 Santa Monica Blvd. Hollywood, Calif. 90069

had his biggest success, after he dispatched him to New Orleans to record a session on the strength of a demo. There, Little Richard sang a wonderfully foul-mouthed ditty on the piano which, once cleaned up, Rupe realised had the makings of a hit single. The result was "Tutti Frutti". With his rampantly effeminate, coiffured demeanour, coupled with uncontainable energy levels, Little Richard is one of both funk and rock's key touchstones and inspirational sources, initiating a lineage that includes Sly Stone, Prince and André 3000 but which also spreads further, and wilder, than that.

The eventual result of this liaison was Ace's Little Richard box set, which covers the astonishingly fertile 13 month period into which Little Richard's series of hits are crammed, with liner notes surveying the career of one of rock'n'roll's most mercurial characters. It's a classic example of Ace's capacity to deliver the complete and finished article in the reissues market.

In 1985, Ace branched into Cajun through a new deal with Floyd Soileau who, in 1958, while just a teenager, opened his first record shop. Descending from a long line of Cajun fiddlers, Soileau eventually began two labels, Swallow Records (based on the pronunciation of his name) and Jin (named after his wife Jinver), as well as further labels dedicated to zydeco recordings. Over the decades, these labels churned out a steady series of noteworthy recordings, including swamp pop recordings such as Rod Bernard's "This Should Go On Forever" and Joe Barry's "I'm A Fool To Care". Cajun 45s had been popular sellers during the market stall days with John Peel, in particular, an avid purchaser and Charlie Gillett's inspirational *Another Saturday Night* compilation on the label, Oval, acting as the way into the music for many. Ace continued issuing Cajun compilations, drawn upon Swallow and other Louisianian labels, with the help of John Broven (another Briton) who was an expert on this repertoire, having written the book *South to Louisiana*.

ABOVE LEFT TO RIGHT:
Adam Herbert and The Playboys; Little Richard's *The Original British Hit Singles*, 1999; and Little Richard's Specialty box set.

GLOBESTYLE
AND
'WORLD MUSIC'

GLOBESTYLE AND 'WORLD MUSIC'

Before the arrival of GlobeStyle Records in 1985—the next addition to Ace's roster of subsidiaries—'world music' had yet to capture the public imagination. That is to say, artists from Africa, Asia and so forth were touring the Western world but interest in them was largely limited to specialists, sonic anthropologists, the still small-scale WOMAD festival and the valiant efforts of John Peel and, increasingly, Andy Kershaw on the peripheries of Radio 1. In 1985, Live Aid's global outreach had been rather embarrassingly dominated by Caucasian, Anglo-American popsters, its logo a rather condescending image of the African continent as the head of a guitar, with a fretboard extending upward from somewhere near Libya. The role of African artists, or indeed those for whom the concert was held, in all of this was relatively mute.

GlobeStyle was the result of consultation between Roger Armstrong and his friend Ben Mandelson (a long-standing associate of Ace Records who had also been a member of Amazorblades during the Chiswick days). Mandelson had played with Orchestra Jazira, the London-based African band, as well as Magazine. He had just started playing in a band called 3 Mustaphas 3, originally conceived to function—in part—as a backing band for overseas

LEFT:
Amazorblades with Ben Mandelson (later friend of 3 Mustapha 3), Chopper (later Oyster Band) and Rob Keyloch (later ace engineer), circa 1970s.

OPPOSITE:
An elegant 3 Mustaphas 3 poster, made at the time of their first album, 1987.

musicians travelling through London. The idea was never fully realised, although 3 Mustaphas 3 did go on to an illustrious career with over three albums for GlobeStyle. They were an immense influence on many of the bands that came after them. Through 3 Mustaphas 3, Mandelson came into working contact with a company that held the rights to the, somewhat laconically named, Super Rail Band of the Buffet Hotel de la Gare de Bamako, Mali.

This was the band that had spawned both Mory Kanté and Salif Keïta, and the snappily titled *New Dimensions in Rail Culture*. This was followed by *Dance Cadence*, a compilation of Zouk music from Guadeloupe and Martinique, issued several years before the Zouk craze. There swiftly followed an album by Lesotho-based band, Puseletso Seema & Tua Ea Linare, presaging the sound of Paul Simon's *Graceland* by several years.

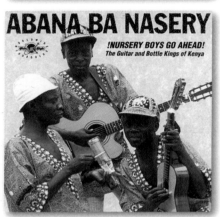

However, even as GlobeStyle was beginning to garner an impressive catalogue, and as interest in non-Anglo-American music was burgeoning (it would not be long before Paul Simon 'discovered' Africa), it occurred to Armstrong that this stuff was difficult to find in the stores. What was needed, frankly, was that thing piously scorned by the musically virtuous—a place to sell the records. Armstrong decided to call a summit meeting:

> Originally Doug Veitch and I got together at the Devonshire Pub one night—he had the Bhundu Boys on his label. With Doug on board, Ben [Mandelson] and I contacted other people that we knew who had labels with similar music and we hired a room above a pub called The Empress of Russia in the Angel. I chaired the meetings and tried to keep it focused on the fact that it was all about a rack in a record shop. Because up until then, if you wanted this music you'd find it in indie, in reggae, in soul, it was all over the place. And to be honest, with Andy [Kershaw] and John [Peel] rattling off the name Abdel Aziz El Mubarak on the radio are you going to pick up on what he just said, or how it's spelt? Are you going to be able to go find that at a record shop the next morning? You needed a rack to go through. I'd worked in retail and I know how shy people are about coming up and saying: 'I heard this record last night and I don't know what it's called.'

So, there it was: 'world music'. The phrase was fatefully and enduringly coined. However, then as now, it has caused a good deal of ambivalence among those who hold the music dearest. Charlie Gillett, for one, endorses the usage of the term: "People are sniffy about it, but it's a category without boundaries or fences. 'World music' could be English-speaking music like gospel or Cajun. Indeed, there are some people who say English folk should be categorised as 'world music' but that's where my own personal fence stays in place, I'm afraid!"

Furthermore, insists Armstrong, whatever misgivings members of the intelligentsia may have had about the moniker, there was no doubting the benefits it brought in terms of exposure to the musicians that fell under its banner: "One small example was that we helped bring in Abana Ba Nasery from Kenya, who consisted of two guys playing guitar and one on a Fanta bottle. They did a mini tour, bought their ghetto blaster, and other goods, and returned home with £500 each in their pockets."

GlobeStyle's first significant hit came not from its African contingent however, but from a less likely, albeit undeniably glamorous source. The late Ofra Haza (of Yemenite heritage) had first come to international fame in 1983, when she came second representing Israel in the Eurovision contest with the song "Hi".

ABOVE TOP TO BOTTOM:
The Super Rail Band of The Buffet Hotel Bamako, 1985, which was the first LP released by GlobeStyle, and Abana Ba Nasery's *Nursery Boys Go Ahead*, 1992.

OPPOSITE:
Ofra Haza in a shot from her breakthrough *Yemenite Songs* album, 1984.

She enjoyed a period as a modest peddler of MOR ('middle of the road') music before a group of Israeli producers approached her with the view to persuading her "back to her roots" and to perform a set of songs based on old Yemenite poetry. In order to popularise the undertaking, an electro remix of one of the songs "Galbi" was commissioned, and the clever combination of beatbox rhythms, samples of Haza's airborne, muezzin vocals, as well as additional strings and percussion, meant that the 12" remix met with some success. Her popularity grew further after the production team, Coldcut, sampled "Im Nin'Alu", the B-side to "Galbi", their efforts then cropping up on the Top 20 hit single "Paid in Full", by hip hop pioneering duo Erik B & Rakim in 1987. As Armstrong recounts:

Grant Goddard, who'd worked with us on press, had been DJing on a pirate radio ship off the coast of Tel Aviv. He found the Ofra Haza LP and it reached us via Charlie. We loved it. We put out a 12" of "Galbi" from the album and got some interest. Normally releases reach a plateau, but this one didn't. Interest continued to build. I remember; we got her onto Woman's Hour, and a big article in *NME* at the same time. We persuaded them to remix "Im Nin'Alu" and what we didn't know is that Coldcut had already used it in the Eric B & Rakim remix, and that became a huge hit. We got daytime play, Radio 1 playlist, right through to Janice Long and John Peel, at which point I realised, this is definitely hot. *Yemenite Songs*, the album she made, is one of our biggest-ever sellers.

GlobeStyle would prove to be another example of Ace providing a springboard for a new artist, only to pass on the baton to less free-thinking, but more commercially geared, operatives in the music business. As 'world music' expanded, Ace's active interest in it paradoxically lessened. "'World music' matured", explains Armstrong. "You really had to be touring acts, needed to deal with agents. It outgrew us, in terms of what we were comfortable doing." Today GlobeStyle is "taking it easy", but it can look back on a heritage that includes not just Ofra Haza, and the first major introduction of Zouk music to these shores, but also the first Bollywood compilations in 1990 (some 15 years in advance of *Bend It Like Beckham* and other such films), an album of Serbian Brass Band music in the 1980s, as well as the Taarab Orchestras of Zanzibar (who had too many members to be brought to Britain—hence the dispatchment of GlobeStyle operatives; Adam Skeaping, Mandelson and Armstrong, armed with a pair of microphones and a digital two-track).

Come 1986 and the advent of CDs, Ace found itself in the strange situation of reissuing its own reissues. However, being already *au fait* with digital technology, Ace was in a better position than most to take advantage of the gradual transfer to the new CD format, and quickly issued Jackie Wilson, Dion & The Belmonts and BB King among others. Ace's pursuit of clean tape sources, impeccably re-mastered, meant the new format was enthusiastically embraced. They could issue these recordings with sound quality never heard outside the studio before.

By the late 1980s, there was a full-swing revival of the 1970s, the decade style had supposedly forgotten. In 1989, Ace licensed Westbound Records of Detroit and acquired Spring Records outright. This meant access to a vast treasure trove of early to mid-1970s funk: Ohio Players, Funkadelic, Detroit Emeralds, the Fatback Band, Joe Simon and Millie Jackson, all acts who to some degree or other suffered from the mechanical onset of disco and its simplistic, sequencer-driven beat.

OPPOSITE:
Globestyle poster from 1987.

ABOVE LEFT TO RIGHT:
Funkadelic's *Maggot Brain*, 1971, and *America Eats Its Young*, 1972.

Armen Boladian started Westbound in 1969 as he moved from distribution into recording. He had, over the years, issued 45s from as early as 1957 with, for example, The Mellotones "Rosie Lee" on his own Fascination Records label. He sold rights to the notorious Morris Levy in what was to prove a salutary lesson in remaining independent. Despite a Top 30 chart position on Gee, Boladian received little payment beyond his advance. After a run of very good Detroit soul group records, Westbound signed up Funkadelic and debuted with "Music for My Mother"—one of the strangest records ever committed to wax. Boladian saw something in the group that others didn't, persevering as they turned the genres of soul and funk inside out to invent an entirely new sound. They became enormously influential and their shows legendary. Westbound also found success with Detroit Emeralds, Ohio Players and Denise La Salle, making them the second biggest label in Detroit, just as the first left home and headed to LA. Boladian was an inspiration for Ace:

> You couldn't wish for a nicer and more co-operative guy to work with than Armen…. Of all those labels and artists we acquired, the ones we do best with are Millie [Jackson] and the Fatback Band. And we're good friends with both Bill Curtis [of Fatback]– he's into his 1970s now but still gigging and drumming—and Millie—she's an absolute gas.

The Fatback Band enjoyed most of their success in the 1970s, with their jazz-elasticated, bassy funk workouts enjoying huge success in the R&B charts (without ever really breaking into the American pop charts). In the late 1970s,

OPPOSITE:
Funkadelic promotional shot, circa 1970s.

ABOVE LEFT TO RIGHT:
Ohio Players' *Ecstasy*, 1973, and Joe Simon promotional shot, circa 1970s.

ACE RECORDS

however, they made innovative plays for a piece of the dance floor action, and had British hits including "Spanish Hustle" and "(Are You Ready) Do the Bus Stop". The Fatback Band defined the term 'anthem' with "I Found Lovin'" in 1984, which they then set Glastonbury alight with in 2004. They are even credited by some scholars of the genre with releasing the first rap single, "King Tim II (Personality Jock)", though this was immediately overshadowed by the rather more obvious "Rapper's Delight" by The Sugarhill Gang, also released in 1979. They revived again in the mid-1980s, with the underrated, conscious, downbeat "Is This The Future?" and still issue the occasional record.

Millie Jackson is a byword for soul ribaldry, however, for all her sauce, she remains one of the great unacknowledged soul queens of her era—to which her concept sequence of albums, commencing with 1974's *Caught Up*, followed by *Still Caught Up*, attest. (All her Spring albums, including these, are available on Ace's Southbound Records label.)

In 1985, having acquired the British rights to one of Fantasy Records' labels, Contemporary Records, Ace went the whole hog and took on their entire catalogue. The relationship with Fantasy was to last over 20 years and would be vitally important in the story of Ace. Access to the huge catalogue gave Ace financial security and allowed the company to generate the money to buy several labels of its own during that period.

Fantasy was largely owned by Ralph Kaffel and Saul Zaentz (who would later produce hit movies including *One Flew Over The Cuckoo's Nest*, *Amadeus* and *The English Patient*). It had started as a small West Coast label with two main assets—Dave Brubeck and the band that was to become Creedence Clearwater Revival (CCR). Over a short period CCR became one of the biggest-selling American groups of all time. Fantasy used the resulting income to purchase several legendary jazz labels including Prestige Records, Milestone Records, Riverside Records and Contemporary, as well as Stax.

Until the late 1980s, Fantasy had licensed its European rights to major labels, including EMI and RCA Records. While they did well with CCR and the bigger Stax artists, vast areas of the catalogue remained untouched and unreleased. Huge overheads and nervous accountants meant that the major labels could only release titles that were guaranteed to sell many thousands of units.

Bill Belmont, head of international licensing at Fantasy, made the same decision that Trevor Churchill had made when licensing Chiswick—choosing

OPPOSITE CLOCKWISE FROM TOP:
The Fatback Band promotional shot, circa 1970s; Millie Jackson's classic *Caught Up* LP, 1974; and Millie Jackson moves with the times into the 1970s.

ABOVE LEFT TO RIGHT:
The Fatback Band's *Six Twelves*, 2003, and *Raising Hell*, 1975.

different labels in each territory rather than one major label to cover the whole of Europe. Crucially, he set up a central manufacturing operation in Germany which meant that each territory could order as many, or as little, as it needed. This avoided the necessity for each country to go through the expensive and time-consuming process of originating each title themselves. As a result, in 2005 the Ace catalogue numbered over 3,000 titles.

Ace was not content with simply releasing the albums pressed in Germany— there were hundreds of other titles that Fantasy had not released on CD that garnered their interest. Over the next two decades they would release the first albums of the acid jazz boom; discover important 'lost' recordings by Stax giants, including such artists as Otis Redding; and, from 1958, even put out interviews with racing drivers.

ABOVE LEFT TO RIGHT:
Westbound's Armen Boladian at the door of the legendary Pac 3 Studio, circa 1980s, and Ralph Kaffel and Bill Belmont of Fantasy Records. Images courtesy of Roger Armstrong.

ACID JAZZ AND THE AND THE GOLDEN AGE

ACID JAZZ AND THE GOLDEN AGE

"We didn't come up with acid jazz but we were the first people to jump on it", says Roger Armstrong of Ace's Beat Goes Public (BGP) label:

> Gilles Peterson said that there was this thing, acid house, doing the rounds—suppose we put this compilation out, call it 'acid jazz', give it a psychedelic cover… fine. Putting out records is cheap. That's the difference between us and a major (where it would have to go before a committee, then a sub-committee, then up to the sales guys for them to say 'no'). It would have floundered. With us, Gilles could suggest the idea and, ten days later, come up with a track listing. It was all Fantasy stuff, which we had exclusive rights to. I ordered up the tapes, went in, cut the record, put it out, and sold a truckload. It was that simple, really.

The mid- to late 1980s were a time of great diffusion in the dance world, with multiple new directions running the gamut from ultra-Modern to Postmodern. Samplers had opened the door on music's history, using a form of technical innovation that disguised the relative lack of forward looking artistic innovation of the era in which it was created. In fields and hangars beyond the M25, Acid House was doing its stripped-bare, Roland 808 thing. Hip hop was in the ascendancy, with Public Enemy, Eric B & Rakim and Run-DMC appealing increasingly to a white rock crowd. Then there were the techno crew, creating minimal dance floor masterpieces out of sonic Meccano. For the more urbane clubber, however, there was a flight to the rich, untapped traditions of the jazz and funk past, couched in the musical idioms of the present day—hence the rise of phenomena like rare groove then acid jazz with DJs, including Peterson, heading the charge.

The name 'acid jazz', which embraced a whole host of decades old genres from Latino, funk, fusion and organ and soul all the way 'up' to jazz itself, was an invention of DJ Chris Bangs. As Dean Rudland, BGP consultant explains: "In the previous six months they'd made about half a dozen attempts to come up with a scene that would stick. Wah wah jazz, and so forth. Then they came up with acid jazz."

BGP was launched and, in 1988, issued *This Is Acid Jazz: Vol 1*, which mostly comprised Hammond organ groups on Prestige who had made up the bulk of Peterson's DJ set at the time—Gene Ammons, Pucho & His Latin Soul Brothers and Leon Spencer. As Armstrong recalls:

What started the whole thing was Gilles saying: 'Do you think people who get into this might subsequently get into jazz?' A 'better' sort of music, as we thought…. Certainly acid jazz helped create and kindle whatever interest there is among young people in jazz. The irony was; those kids then started making acid jazz records and were the first generation in a while to have shown any great love for jazz. And they would tell you all about the attitude of the hardcore record shops in London—they looked down their noses as these snotty youths who didn't know the matrix number of some Miles Davis record.

Distrusted by the jazz purists, there were, conversely, those who believed that acid jazz fans were taking refuge from the present day in the cosy authenticity of the musical past. Not so, says Rudland:

That scene was seen as purely retro by people on the outside but, from 1989–1992, it was playing mostly brand new records. You had a period when American hip hoppers like A Tribe Called Quest were coming over to London, buying records out of Soul Jazz in Soho, taking them back, sampling them, and then I was buying these hip hop records at On The Beat in Greek Street. The music had come a huge, full circle. It was phenomenally exciting for a while, the sort of scene I'd dreamt of, but one that became very formulaic and boring once the hits started flowing.

The acid jazzers were the inheritors of a 1960s mod sensibility. Rudland was an aficionado of the type of soul artefacts beloved by 1960s mods, before moving to the WAG Club, Soho, and immersing himself in the emergent acid jazz scene:

The other connection is The Prisoners, who were this incredible garage band on Big Beat in the mid-1980s. James Taylor, later of The James Taylor Quartet, was their organist. He nearly signed to Ace, before signing to Polydor. It kind of revolves around those two aspects, one of which emphasises the garage/mod side of acid jazz.

Peterson eventually left BGP to head up Talkin' Loud and, while the original acid jazz scene would yield Jamiroquai and Brand New Heavies in the 1990s, it did eventually become a little bland. However, at Ace, BGP ploughed a different furrow—a 1994 live jazz dance event featuring the old school Idris Muhammad, Eddie Pazant and Reuben Wilson, under the prosaic heading "Make Way For The Originals". As ever, the eventual hit makers of a scene Ace helped inaugurate were elsewhere.

Today, acid jazz has joined doo-wop, R&B, rock'n'roll, and so on, in the pantheon of musical history, another genre to be mined for reissue. However, this has also brought about its own problems. "Now that we're looking at the old Acid Jazz [the label not the 'genre'] catalogue, it's really freaky", says Rudland:

> We've just worked on the reissue of one of the acid jazz albums, a band called Mother Earth and an album called *The People Tree*. That was an epic work. I had to go up to Ed's [Piller, the album's producer] house in Harlow to go through the tapes. And it was an experience totally akin to looking through the tapes of some 1950s/60s indie label from America—cobwebs everywhere, reels and reels of tape, absolute craziness.

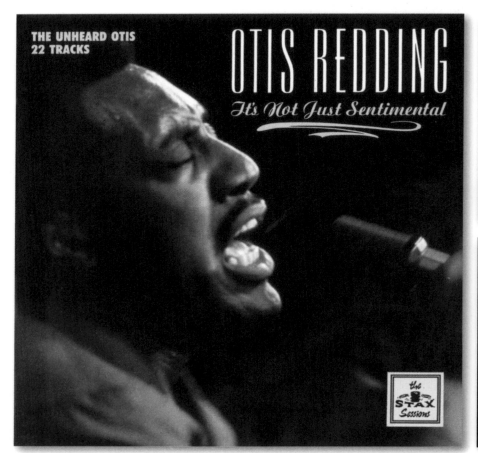

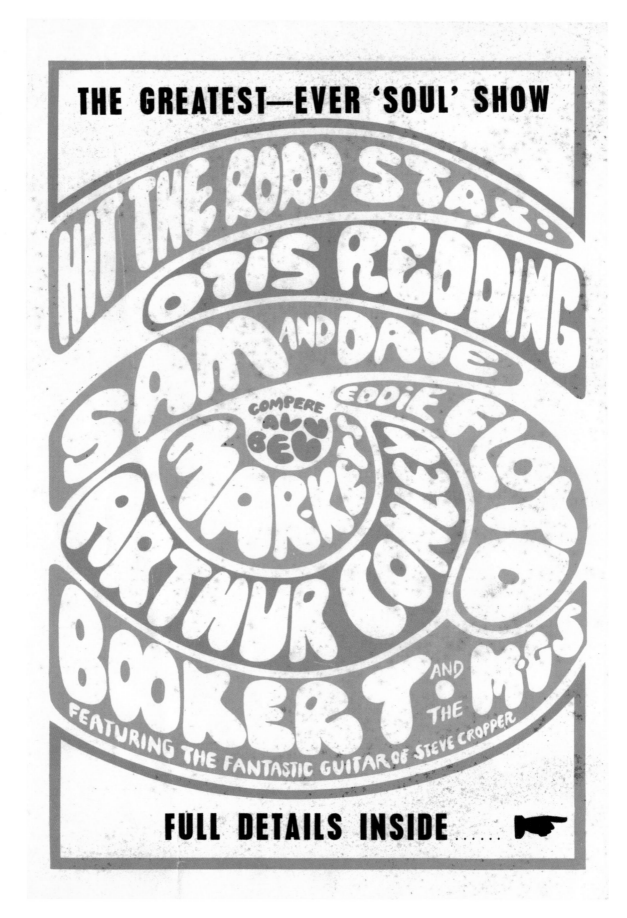

I've always had a very historical, analytical retrospective attitude towards music. But then, when it comes to something I was involved in 13, 14 years ago.... We brought out this mix down tape, and there's this backing singer on it. And we're all, like: 'What? Who is it? Who was she?' Me and Ed didn't remember her, Matt [Deighton, the lead singer]—no recollection. So then, you're getting guys in America to sit down and recall events from 40 years ago.... They were operating in a period where this stuff was considered throwaway and they had no idea some bloke like me would be coming along and peppering them with questions about it four decades down the line.

Stax presented both the most exciting and the most daunting prospect for Ace's team to dig through. The label was formed by a white country fiddle player, Jim Stewart—in Memphis in the late 1950s—and started life issuing hillbilly and rockabilly music. Stewart was the victim/beneficiary of 'white flight', as the neighbourhood in which his studio was based became increasingly populated by black Americans. Consequently the label switched to the more lucrative option of R&B, with acts like Rufus and Carla Thomas, The Mar-Keys and Booker T and The MG's, developing what would be perceived as the signature sound of the label—raw, meaty and impassioned, a Southern-fried antithesis to the slicker sounds emanating from the labels and studios of their North American counterparts. (It is said that this sound was created by accident, the result of the acoustics in the lopsided theatre in which Stax's studios were based.) A distribution deal between Jerry Wexler's Atlantic Records and the label led to a mutual cross-fertilisation of artists and opportunities, involving Wilson Pickett, Sam & Dave and Otis Redding. Post-Atlantic the label went from strength to strength but, despite hugely successful landmark recordings like Isaac Hayes' "Hot Buttered Soul" (or perhaps because of them), Stax went bankrupt in 1974.

Following an initial flurry of vinyl-only re-releases, including a series of 20 45s and "Hot Buttered Soul", in 1990 and 1991, Armstrong undertook a huge research programme into the Stax vaults, courtesy of Fantasy, transferring some 130 hours of early Atlantic period Stax material to DAT. (Armstrong still gets goosebumps as he recalls hearing the multi-track session tape for Otis Redding's "Dock of the Bay" that had not been heard by anyone since the day the record was made.) These tape trawls also produced whole albums of unissued material by Booker T and The MG's, Rufus and Carla Thomas, William Bell, Ruby Johnson and Mable John—one of two acts to record for both Stax and Motown.

In 1991, the first volume of *The Golden Age of American Rock'n'Roll* was issued on Ace. It covered the period from 1954–1963, when rock'n'roll burst onto the scene in a fully formed state of adolescence—a state that was sustained until the early 1960s. The series has now reached its own 'teens'—it is among Ace's best-selling compilations—and has sprouted numerous offshoots along the way. "We felt we were running out of road at Volume Ten", says Ace consultant and liner note writer Rob Finnis. "But we stretched to Volume 11 and then still beyond with various genre compilations like the novelty and doo-wop ones."

This series is compiled by Trevor Churchill (with John Broven as an adjunct) and Finnis who, as a very young man, had made that groundbreaking odyssey across America in the 1960s, to meet and interview the still relatively young—if somewhat neglected members—of the early rock'n'roll pantheon. Part of the reason for the success of the series, Finnis believes, is his own, relatively commercial sensibility: "I think to myself, will this sell? In a way, it's coldly clinical but also, I wouldn't want to waste Ace's money."

 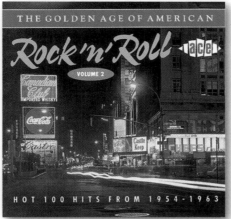 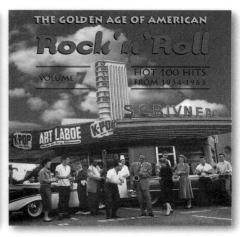

However, *The Golden Age of American Rock'n'Roll* series is no mere nostalgia fest for elderly, Brylcreemed types confused by the innovations in rock since the release of "I Want to Hold Your Hand". As one chastened fan put it: "If, like me, you thought you had a comprehensive collection of American music from the late 1950s to the early 1960s, you may have to think again." The first volume contains "Louie Louie" by The Kingsmen and "Let's Dance" by Chris Montez (a British hit when reissued in the early 1970s), as well as "Denise" by Randy & The Rainbows which later became a hit for Blondie as "Denis". Although these singles are familiar to many today, the original compilation brief was, says Finnis: "Not to put out stuff that was too easily available [on CD]—avoid the Jerry Lees. It also was to find the best quality tape source possible—so even if you've got the track on something else, you'll never have heard it this good before."

So the series concentrates on records that are hard to find on CD. The rock'n'roll era was an astonishingly fecund period, in which vocal groups—greased back, craggy instrumental rockers like Link Wray, bouffant girlie popsters, twisters, novelty hits-ters, lovelorn teen crooners and R&B crossover acts—all jostled together, in a crowded scene energised by the emergence of cheap and quick fire indie labels able to catch talent in a way in which the staid corporate labels could not. A surprisingly large number of these relatively obscure records were issued in Britain, but mostly disappeared through lack of radio play. Rock'n'roll was anathema to the BBC, still hidebound by dreary, Reithian austerity even as the 1960s were beginning to take hold.

Taking *The Golden Age of American Rock'n'Roll: Volume 2*, as an example, what is striking (even to those accustomed to the genres in which these young acts were performing) is the frantic, libidinous quality of their vocals, the sheer release of energy that is out of proportion to the arrangements they're working off—be it the exchanges between Billy Bland and the female vocalist on "Let the Little Girl Dance", or the unexpected falsetto surge of "Stay" by Maurice Williams & The Zodiacs, (which, incidentally, clocking in at one minute, 36 seconds, is the shortest number one single of all time). "Junkman" is a pink, oestrogen burst of harmonic infatuation, full of promise of things to come. But then, the hits come from all methods, all directions. Take The Silhouettes' "Get a Job" which, once it had struggled to get a national distribution deal, was a massive hit—its supposedly 'wacky' but actually cleverly crafted doo-wop scat a cover for its hard times lyrical theme.

OPPOSITE:
Ace relaunched Stax Records in 1987 with 20 45s. This is the familiar logo with which they were associated.

ABOVE LEFT TO RIGHT:
The Golden Age of American Rock'n'Roll Vol 10, 2004—Ace Records' long running and most successful series to date; *The Golden Age of American Rock'n'Roll: Vol 2*, 1993; and *The Golden Age of American Rock'n'Roll: Vol 7*, 1998.

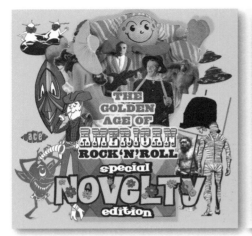  

What is vital to the *Golden Age* series, both to its success and an understanding of its contents and context, are the liner notes by Finnis—telling the back story to often long-forgotten artists, whose bequest to posterity might otherwise be one-off perforated, black and white press shots. Finnis' notes convey the engrossing, bittersweet tales of how these records came to be made, the rise and fall of the artists' success and the, often accidental, afterlives of the songs. "It could be some guy from the sticks who makes a record just for the local market and it's a hit and suddenly he's out of his depth", says Finnis:

> Something like "Sea of Love" by Phil Phillips (a big hit in 1959), a very primitive record recorded in a backroom shack—that became a big seller again because of the Al Pacino film 30 years later (also called *Sea of Love*)—these things have lives of their own, you never quite know where they're going.

The stories are minute and manifold, with the odd lapse into the *demimonde* from which so much rock'n'roll evolved. There were characters like John Dolphin, the black entrepreneur from South Central LA, wont to take songwriting credits under the pseudonym of J Gray. "Buzz Buzz Buzz", credited to this pseudonym, was a big hit for The Hollywood Flames, although Dolphin did not live to see the rewards—he was shot dead in his own office by one Percy Ivy, a disgruntled songwriter to whom he allegedly owed money. Another such example is The Bell Notes, whose single "I Had It" was adamantly claimed by veteran songwriter Ellie ("Be My Baby") Greenwich as her own—allegedly performed at amateur hops near her home in Long Island. Kenny Dino is another, whose oddly effective Elvis-impersonating "Your Ma Said You Cried in Your Sleep Last Night" was so loathed by the head honcho at the record label, he picked up the copy played to him and threw it against the wall. Dino didn't like the song either, yet eventually it found a release, became a number 24 pop hit in America, and now survives on CD.

It is no coincidence that this era came to an abrupt halt around 1963, when the onset of Beatlemania buried all that had preceded it. Yet, because they inadvertently obliterated so much, there remains so much to discover. So popular has the *Golden Age* series proven, that it has spawned numerous offshoots, including country, doo-wop and novelty record collections. Its popularity also serves as a reminder that, back in that *Golden* era, it was by no means certain that rock, of the 'n' roll variety, was going to become the dominant genre of the future. And so, the past stretches before us, unknown....

ABOVE LEFT TO RIGHT:
The Golden Age of American Rock'n'Roll Special Novelty Edition, 2003; *The Golden Age of American Rock'n'Roll Special Doo-Wop Edition,* 2004; and *The Golden Age of American Rock'n'Roll Special Country Edition,* 2002.

SONNY FISHER TOUR POSTER, 1980S.

Sonny Fisher pioneered the sound of rockabilly in his unique fusion of country and blues music. At the offset he received only marginal success, however, when Ace released a number of his recordings from the 1950s, he swiftly gained the moniker 'king of the rockabilly revival'.

SONNY FISHER

U.K. Tour 1980

Singles:
NS 54 Pink & Black/Sneaky Pete 45rpm
NST 59 Rockin' Daddy/I Can't Lose 78rpm

UK Representation:
PAUL BARRET
0222 704279

THE ESCALATORS PROMOTIONAL STICKER, CIRA 1980S.

Creators of "Dog Eat Robot" and "Eskimo Rock", The
Escalators comprised of two former members of the rockabilly
project, The Meteors, who would later go on to form another
Ace group, the Tall Boys.

WHIRLWIND PROMOTIONAL STICKER, CIRCA 1970S.

This sticker humourously plays on the name of the band as
well as serving as a reminder of their rockabilly roots.

PINNACLE RECORDS' CUDDLY BEAR ADVERTISEMENT, 1984

A promotional poster advertising the British comedy version of "Teddy Bear" by Ike and Tina Turner.

AMAZORBLADES PROMOTIONAL STICKER, CIRCA 1970S.

This punchy and colourful design reflects the Amazorblades own punk repertoire. As the band only had a hit with one release—"Common Truth" on Chiswick—this is a rare example of their promotional material.

CATALOGUE NOVEMBER 1983

CATALOGUE JAN '85

ACE RECORDS LTD

ace

CD

CATALOGUE

autumn 1987

ACE · BIG BEAT · KENT ·
IMPACT · GLOBESTYLE ·
FANTASY · BOPLICITY ·
CONTEMPORARY · STAX

OPPOSITE TOP: ACE RECORDS CATALOGUE, 1983.

This front cover for this 1983 catalogue was, quite possibly, a satirical reference to the label's humble beginnings in the form of the Rock On shop in the 1970s (and might also have been an attempt to communicate that their principals were still very much prevalent, despite their increasing success). It also repeats the motif used in the championed *Ace Story* volumes, some of the labels most successful albums to date.

OPPOSITE BOTTOM: ACE RECORDS CATALOGUE, 1985.

This 1985 catalogue is a reminder of the recent acquisition of the Kent label, which would not only introduce Ace to Ady Croasdell (aka Harboro Horace) but also set in motion the burgeoning northern soul scene in the Britain. Some of the most renowned artists included in the catalogue would be Rocky Sharpe & The Replays, Radio Stars and Sniff 'n' the Tears.

LEFT: FIRST ACE RECORDS CD CATALOGUE, 1987.

This first CD catalogue, produced just a few years after the label's inception, already demonstrated the wealth of its oeuvre. Encompassing such labels as Big Beat, Kent, GlobeStyle and Stax, those who flicked through its pages would come across a number of releases by such seminal artists as BB King, Elmore James and Ike and Tina Turner as well as a number of recordings contemporary to the day.

BILLY 'F' GIBBONS
HOLLYWOOD - CALIFORNIA

JULY 18.1994

LONDRES

MR. ROGER ARMSTRONG, MR. TED CARROLL
AND, MR. RAY TOPPING

ACE RECORDS,LTD.
46-50 STEELE ROAD,
NW10 7 AS,
UK

SIRS:

SENDIN' A NOTE OF APPRECIATION FOR THE IMMENSE AND INTENSE 'ROUND-TH'-TOWN 'THRASH',
WHILE THE BUZZ OF 'R & B' SET A GROOVE-TONE TO TIP-TII'-TRIP! WAY 'FINE'!!! WAY 'FINE'.

MILLION THANKS.

AND...A SPECIAL ACKNOWLEDGEMENT WITH THE MOST GRACIOUS HOSPITALITY CITED FOR THE
'VIP'...(!)...VISIT THRU YOUR WORLDLY-RENOWNED ROOFLINED, 'RACKS-O'-RECORDINGS.

YOUR 'OUTFIT'S', MOST DEFINATELY, TOPS. THRASH-MASH-BASH, ONWARD & FORWARD, AS IT'S
  "SAID"!!!
'TIL LATER & SOONER,TOO...(!)..."STAY COOL"...(!)...(!).

KINDEST PERSONAL RECARDS,

MR. BILLY 'F' GIBBONS
dsptch:H'WOODCA 00890060101

COSMETICS — FINE GUITARS — MEDICINES
EXTRACTS — BLUES RECORDINGS — CURIOS
HOUSEHOLD GOODS — JEWELRY

VARIOUS ACE RECORDS BADGES.

Now extremely sought after, these badges can often be found selling on eBAY from £5 upward. Other accessories that the label produces include limited edition T-shirts, featuring Goldwax and Mirwood logos, as well as a commemorative twenty-fifth anniversary Kent design.

OPPOSITE: LETTER FROM BILLY 'F' GIBBONS TO ROGER ARMSTRONG, TED CARROLL AND RAY TOPPING, 1994.

This emphatic letter was from Billy 'F' Gibbons (also known as Reverend Willie G), best known as the guitarist, and some time lead vocalist, for ZZ Top.

15, Northland Way,
L' DERRY,
N' IRELAND.
25-3-78

Dear Chiswick Records,
We have sent you a recording of "The Undertones". We come from Derry in Ireland but don't let that put you off.
The band is
John O'Neill = Rhythm Guitar   age   20
Deemented   = Lead   "   "   16
Micky Bradley = Bass   "   "   18
Feargal Sharkey = Singing   "   18
Billy Doherty   = Drums   "   18
The demo tape contains some of our songs as we hadn't the time or money to record them all. There are a few mistakes due to circumstances beyond our control (the man kept telling us to hurry up). We would very much like it if we could make a record.
We have enclosed an S.A.E.
Please could you reply as soon as possible.

Yours Sincerely
Billy Doherty.

Telephone Derry: 0504, 62690
                    OR
          0504, 66848

P. S: We have included photographs of the band.
      All the songs are our own.

LETTER AND PHOTOGRAPH FROM BILLY DOHERTY (OF THE UNDERTONES) TO CHISWICK, 1978.

This letter accompanied the demo tape The Undertones sent to Chiswick Records. It details the band members, their ages (ranging from 16–20), a photograph and charmingly asks for a record deal.

COVER FOR THE LYRICS AND MUSIC OF "FEVER" BY LITTLE WILLIE JOHN, CIRCA 1950S.

This iconic song would be made famous by Ella Fitzgerald's version of it, as well as being covered by Peggy Lee (1958) and by Rita Coolidge (1973). Willie John's version would chart at number 24 in 1956.

THE ROXY CLUB MEMBERSHIP CARD, 1977.

This membership card entitled the holder to privileged entry into The Roxy, the club known for flowering the early British punk scene in the mid to late 1970s. This particular card belonged to Ace director, Roger Armstrong.

ACE RECORDS CHANGE OF ADDRESS FLYER.

This card was issued during the label's move to Grafton Road in Kentish Town in the mid-1980s.

THE IKETTES "PEACHES 'N' CREAM" PROMOTIONAL POSTER, CIRCA 1960S.

This poster was created to promote Peaches and Cream, the top 40 hit that helped the Ikettes—who started out in the music world as the backing vocalists for The Ike and Tina Revue—establish themselves as a musical force in their own right.

TIME OUT INVITATION TO FIRST NIGHT OUT, CIRCA 1970S.

The Global Village in the 1970s was a popular venue frequented by, mostly working class, kids from the London suburbs—all seriously into their rock'n'roll, rockabilly and R&B. Among those bands they would have been able to see at 'First Night Out' were Chiswick favourites Rocky Sharpe and the Razors and The Count Bishops.

DEEP SOUL

In 1997, the first volume of a series of deep soul was issued on Kent Records. Responsible for compiling them was Dave Godin, a bespectacled, bearded fellow who stared unsmilingly at you from a photo in the booklet accompanying the album. Godin was a vegan, an ardent socialist, founder of the Anvil Cinema in Sheffield, an Esperanto speaker, animal rights activist, atheist (although he was also a member of his local pro-life movement), latterly a student of Jainism (the ancient Indian religion which believed that the mind resides not in the brain but in the heart) and a chain smoker who died in 2004, of lung cancer.

Godin was as ardent a champion of soul music as Britain has ever produced, the founder of the Tamla Motown Appreciation society who would personally greet Motown artists as they stepped off the plane and onto British soil (when he visited the label himself in America, he was greeted on the steps of Motown HQ by Berry Gordy and his entire staff). He was the man credited with introducing Mick Jagger to soul music (though when he heard how Jagger had used it, he wished he hadn't), a record shop owner and, as a music journalist, the man who coined the phrases "northern soul" and then "deep soul".

Godin's name was appended to the four Kent volumes of *Deep Soul Treasures* he compiled, the first of which was one of Ace's best selling compilation CDs to date. "He was intense about everything he did from smoking himself to death to animal rights to socialism—he was a socialist to his death", recalls Ady Croasdell:

> He had his own, very particular idea of what deep soul was. We'd been talking about doing this deep soul compilation for years and when we did, it was a bit like extracting teeth. Dave was very definite about what he wanted but you have licensing restrictions, sometimes you can't find who owns things. Still, we persevered… and when it did come out, Dave just got on the phone—he rang everybody. He was a great self-promoter but, in so doing, he was promoting the record, which was part of his body and soul. And to be fair to him, he was the guy who put that thing on the map—that, and, of course, the fact that the music was so wonderful.

Even those close to Godin, particularly those who worked with him, would agree that Godin could be somewhat "over the top". Yet his sleeve notes for these compilations, overheated as they are, are infectious in their hyperbole and, more importantly, fully borne out by the music contained therein. "Dave Godin was a pioneering spirit", says Croasdell, whose job, as Godin was always anxious to point out, was to do much of the legwork in terms of licensing the various tracks for these anthologies:

> He dropped out of the scene after some of its internal politics—then re-emerged after exile and wanted to put out this defining collection. For him, deep soul meant that the performance had to be very emotional, tragic even. And I agreed with him, it didn't matter where it was cut, whether it was New York or in the Deep South. It was the intensity that mattered.

OPPOSITE LEFT TO RIGHT;
Roy Hamilton's "The Dark End of The Street", from Dave Godin's Deep Soul label. Image courtesy of The Dave Godin Archive. *Dave Godin's Deep Soul Treasures* (volumes 1–4). Dave Godin's life's work in soul music summed up in these massive selling CDs.

ABOVE:
Dave Godin and Marvin Gaye looking exceptionally cool, circa 1970s. Image courtesy of The Dave Godin Archive.

Godin's sleeve notes for the first *Deep Soul* compilation was like a manifesto. He spoke of the music as the "logical, natural and unfeigned successor to the blues", a music that "set its face against emotional compromise". He hinted strongly at the deeply held belief that such music was forged in the privations and civil disadvantages still suffered by many black Americans in the mid-1960s and that these songs—though they were primarily love songs—could be perceived as covert 'protest' songs in their melancholy and anguish (what students of black American music often describe as "masking"). However, he saw deep soul as more universal in its scope and traditions, comparing it to the catharsis of Greek tragedy (by its ability to enable those who saw it to recognise the painfulness of the human condition without having to experience it first hand). Indeed, deep soul, despite its frequent, implacable despondency, appeals precisely because its arrangements, its exquisitely excavated vocal performances, ooze bliss from every pore.

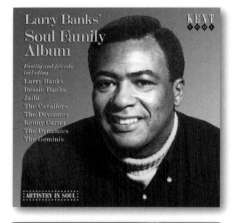

Most the artists featured on the first *Deep Soul Treasures* CD were not household names. Indeed, the most recognisable name is that of Barry White, who takes a compositional co-credit on Brendetta Davis' "I Can't Make it Without Him". However, so unsparingly superlative are each and every one of these tracks that they not only call into question the system which apportions so much attention to so few artists, but also highlights that talent can be abundant rather than scarce.

Among the treasures here are Timmy Willis' "Easy As Saying 1-2-3", a Stax-style outing which, true to deep soul tenets, is dramatically unresolved. "Lights Out" by Zerben R Hicks & The Dynamics, set to the looming backdrop of a militaristic beat, is an early, 1967 example of the profound misgivings about the Vietnam War, especially among the young black men largely sent to Vietnam to wage it. Tracks by Larry Banks, the heart-meltingly orchestrated "I'm Not the One" and Jimmy Holiday's "The Turning Point" also exhibit a delicacy and generosity of feeling towards women which hasn't always been in such evidence in more recent strains of music such as hip hop, for example. Eddie & Ernie's "I'm Goin' for Myself", meanwhile, is a song about solitude, or of the heartbroken man's determination to follow a solo, loveless path.

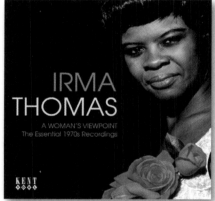

But it's the female artists themselves who provide some of the finest moments on this anthology. Irma Thomas made two takes of "Anyone Who Knows What Love Is (Will Understand)". This was 1964, just as recording was on the cusp of going stereo—and for the album on which this eventually appeared, she had to re-record the song in the latter format. This was much to her chagrin, as she felt she had given pretty much everything she had got into the mono performance. Godin certainly noticed the difference. He observed that, on the stereo version, Thomas adds a "just" to the original lyric, "I feel so sorry for the ones who pity me". That "just" he considered evidence of emotional equivocation, anathema to deep soul, an indication that Thomas regarded the re-rendering of the song as a chore. He therefore, quite unabashedly, took all pains to ensure that Ace/Kent moved heaven and earth to secure and use the mono recording for this compilation. Such diligence, however onerous for those who had to deal with its practical consequences, was crucial. The line cited above is among the most powerful in all of those recordings.

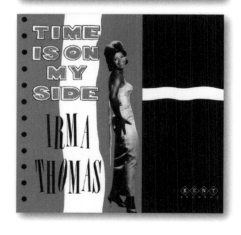

Finally, there was Jaibi, whose 1967 side "You Got Me" Godin reserves for the end of this collection, and which he describes, with typical restraint, as "without doubt or any reservation, my favourite record of all time" and "the ultimate in soul music". There is a certainly truth to this—stately and measured

in its arrangement and delivery, Jaibi's cascading vocal captures the impassioned ambivalence of the heart's conflicting desire for both freedom and captivity.

Sadly, the personal lives of a number of the deep soul artists matched the melancholy of their music. Jaibi died of leukaemia in the 1990s, while Edgar Campbell of Arizona duo Eddie & Ernie died in 1994, aged just 54. His partner survived long enough to see the benefits of Godin's efforts in bringing such material to light (material which, unbeknown to both its writers and performers, he had managed to preserve for many years). Croasdell remembers a broken Ernie in the 1990s, pushing his worldly goods about in a trolley, completely oblivious to the fact that, thousands of miles away, dedicated collectors were paying up to £1,000 a go for rare Eddie & Ernie singles. As another project in Phoenix brought Ernie face to face with Ace representatives, Croasdell recalls the artist being overcome with emotion on hearing of such revived interest:

He was just happy that their work was appreciated, that he wasn't a loser, that in Europe that there were people who considered him a genius. No one in Phoenix really knew who he was. The other thing you've got to look at is, America judges success or failure in purely commercial terms, In America, if you didn't sell any

Larry Banks' Soul Family Album, 2007—a Dave Godin spin off; Irma Thomas' *A Woman's Viewpoint*, 2006; and *Time is on My Side*, 1996.

ABOVE:
Eddie & Ernie, circa 1960s, who featured on *Dave Godin's Deep Soul Treasures* series. Image courtesy of Ernie Johnson.

records, your record's a flop, you're a loser. In Britain and Europe, we didn't know if a record was a hit, we examined these records on their merits.

Godin went on to issue three more deep soul combinations and, though the emphasis shifted on some of them (to up-tempo or more widely-known tracks by the likes of Bobby Womack), they maintained their exceptionally high standard, unearthing more pearls such as The Premiers' "Make it Me", a weirdly halting, shamanistic offering co-written by Isaac Hayes, or Loretta Williams' "I'm Missing You". There was no photo of Williams, and so far as Godin knew, she had no idea that this record, after which she made no known other, was being reissued.

"Dave knew that his selections were esoteric and certainly had no illusions that these things would reach the Top 10", says Ady Croasdell. "He didn't expect the project to make any money... he was just thankful we'd taken on the project and refused to take a compiler's fee for the first one, even when it became the success it did. He was a man of huge principles."

Certainly, in a contemporary pop world dominated by turgid power ballads blasted out by heavily mannered, histrionic vocalists, these deep soul compilations come as a raw yet accomplished relief. As music editor for *The Observer*, Caspar Llewellyn Smith wrote, these records "stand outside the vagaries of the pop market". Moreover, as the great Bettye LaVette noted, in a written tribute to Dave Godin: "He has added years to my artistic life." "In an illustrious life", says Croasdell, "he considered getting *Deep Soul Treasures* out his finest achievement."

ABOVE:
Garnet Mimms, circa 1960s, who featured on *Dave Godin's Deep Soul Treasures* series.

LICENSING—A TOUGH, DIRTY JOB

Speaking recently in an interview with online magazine *The Lance Monthly*, former Stingray, Alec Palao, illustrated just how Ace differs from other record companies when it comes to the surprisingly messy, strenuous and protracted business of licensing and label acquisition. He and Ted Carroll had been working on purchasing the rights to a pair of LA-based independent labels that held a great deal of material from the 1950s and 60s. "The master tapes to these labels were in the garage of the deceased owner, covered in mould and dirt", recollected Palao. "Many tapes were in water-damaged boxes, or out of their boxes entirely. The entire space looked like a hurricane had hit it, and it was, to be frank, a disgusting mess."

According to the family of the owner, Ace were not the only reissues label to have paid a visit with a view to acquiring these labels. However, as soon as the garage door had been lifted and they beheld the mess contained therein, the other enquirers had made their apologies and left. Not Carroll and Palao. As Carroll remarked, they were like "pigs in shit", and were soon down in the

detritus, sleeves rolled up, rummaging for doo-wop, surf and instrumental rock, soul and rockabilly—material that, Palao believes, no other label would know what to do with, even if they could bear to pick through the mess in order to get to it.

"'Licensing' sounds very dry, as if it's just sitting down and signing a piece of paper", says Roger Armstrong. However, there is a great deal more to it than that. Fingers are broken, blisters developed and calluses nurtured after the countless hours of crate digging, vinyl browsing, paper sorting and filing. For Ace consultants such as Peter Gibbon, Dean Rudland, Tony Rounce and Ady Croasdell, the whole licensing process has involved frequent transatlantic slogs, knocking on the doors of perfect strangers, of receiving late night telephone calls from those American labels oblivious to global time differences. It involves competing with bootleggers, haggling with naive representatives from corporate record companies, spending far too much time in warehouses and being reprimanded for knocking over the organ that Sam the Sham played on "Woolly Bully".

"We worry these things into existence, and fret after they have been released, in case anything isn't quite as it should be", says Armstrong of the long process whereby Ace compilations and reissues come into being. "It's all a lot more involved than people imagine—especially the complex [releases] like Dave Godin's *Deep Soul Treasures*, where you're licensing maybe 18–20 people, or 24 tracks off 24 different people."

Gibbon is responsible for maintaining and creating the label's huge database, keeping record of the tracks it either owns or has already released, together with an enormous singles discography. When Ace acquire a new record company such as the Hollywood label, Dore for example, it falls to him to incorporate not just the tapes but also the, often incomplete, paperwork —a process that often involves piecing records together in a manner which he refers to as "forensic discography".

Over the years, master books, label copy and other documentation can go missing. Sometimes they are accidentally disposed of, on other occasions they

OPPOSITE LEFT TO RIGHT:
Two CDs illustrated by Mitch O'Connell and featuring tracks from the Downey Records catalogue (a label from Southern California recently acquired by Ace and home of the original issue of The Chantays' "Pipeline", the definitive surf record).

ABOVE:
(Left to right) Peter Gibbon, Ray Topping, Rob Hughes and John Broven at one of the annual consultants meetings, circa 1990s. Image courtesy of Roger Armstrong.

have been consumed by fire, or even spirited away due to tax and financial investigations. So the forensic nature of the task comes from piecing together the information about a company from what is left—boxes of invoices and associated material.

"I've been going through the receipts of Dore, one of latest acquisitions", explains Gibbon:

> Everybody thinks that there's a convenient bundle of information about the company but it's rarely the case. I've got to try and pull it all together from boxes of old paperwork. Sometimes, for example, linking information on a pressing plant's invoice with master numbers scrawled on a tape box is the way we figure out what recordings we've actually got.

However, surprising aspects of record business operations spring out of these investigations, as Gibbon outlines:

> Record companies pay for specialist firms to master their records from tapes and to produce the metalwork and stampers that are then used to press the records. The stampers had to be shipped to the pressing plants and the record company was charged for this. Well, that's OK if the mastering company is in LA and the pressing plant is in New York State, but I've just discovered from these receipts that Dore were being charged for shipment of stampers to a local pressing plant. Not only was it in LA, but the address of the plant was that of the side door in the very same building!

ABOVE CLOCKWISE FROM LEFT:
Bobby Freeman signs with Syd Nathan at King Records, circa 1970s. Image courtesy of King Records, Inc. *King Rockabilly*, 2001; and *King Rock'n'Roll*, 2003.

As well as dealing with the giant boxes of paperwork that fetch up at Ace's northwest London canal-side headquarters, Gibbon has served his time running up and down ladders in giant, hangar-sized warehouses in America—where long-neglected product sat in rows across a multitude of vast shelves, all patiently awaiting rediscovery and restoration. "One day I was in a warehouse in Austin, Texas", recalls Gibbon:

> There must have been a million records in there. There was a film crew there, while I was scrabbling around, and they decided they wanted to interview me. They saw this wish list I was holding…. The cameraman is at my shoulder, he points at random at a record on my list and he says: 'How long have you been looking for that record?' I say, '25 years'. And he says: 'What's it like?' I say: 'I don't know. I've never heard it.' And at this point the whole of the crew cracked up laughing. I never had the opportunity to explain to them that this was a small Chicago label [and] all the records on it were by the same production team, not a duffer among them, so the chances are this would be a gem too.

In 2005, Ace was given access to King Records, a Cincinnati-based label set up by Syd Nathan, which specialised first in country, then in rockabilly and R&B. It was Rounce's job to see the project through from beginning to end, starting at the King storage facilities. "These acetates had been shelved, quite literally—sitting in a corner of the King tape room waiting for someone to come and listen to them", says Rounce:

> And the thing is, these acetates are fragile. When we bought Modern Records, a great deal of their repertoire was on acetate. They'd been looked after to a certain extent but once tape came in, I think the attitude was, 'well, this music's here today and gone tomorrow anyway, we won't throw these things away but we won't be looking at them very often'. So they'd get stacked badly, they'd get grime in the grooves, they'd get scratched, bits would fall off them and because they're acetone-based, they start to sweat—and they give off some really horrible fumes. The King acetates are in remarkably good condition, but while working on them back in London, I've often had to go and have a lie down because I've been too close to the source and I'm, like, is this Wednesday or is my name Malcolm? Fortunately, we have the technology to clean up the sound of an acetate and that is essentially as good as putting you on the floor of the studio with the original artist and band.

Ray Topping, Ace's first consultant, wrote of his experiences tracking down master tapes and material—of entering derelict buildings with shelves littered with press shots of soul artists nibbled away by rats, or of going to one of the modern archives in South Central LA, copying masters reel-to-reel and returning home only to realise the tapes he'd made had become ruined by phantom police messages. He also recalled a trip to the Music Corporation of America (MCA) vaults in Los Angeles in search of Duke and Peacock master tapes, only to discover that the ladder he had been given did not reach the top two shelves where they were stored. "I was determined not to be defeated and stacked boxes on top of the ladder so I could reach the elusive masters", he recounts. "Luckily I didn't fall off and break my neck."

Despite the physical dangers to which the crack Ace team subject themselves in the quest to rescue ancient rockabilly, R&B, and so on, from the deathly clutches of oblivion, licensing individual tracks from bigger record companies is fraught with its own pitfalls—the least of which is the ignorance of the companies themselves. "People think we write out a list of the tracks we'd like, and then a compilation automatically pops up and we all go down the pub", says Gibbon:

> But it's much, much more complicated than that; it's a challenge. One of the main problems we've got is that some of this old music is buried in the mists of time and we have to spend a lot of time trying to persuade the companies that they actually own this music and that it exists in the first place. We're talking about 40–50 year old music while the person responsible for licensing it might only be 28. To them, it's an abstract name and number and if the 'computer says no'…. The irony is, we're paying them to do all this.

While the larger record companies don't appear to be getting any wiser, they are getting warier, it seems. "15, 20 years ago it was easier to license", Gibbon continues: "But now, they're worried about litigation and if there isn't contractual paperwork, they're wary about putting it out. It gets harder, not easier, as time goes on. And we still go through the motions of licensing things despite the fact that some of the copyrights have lapsed."

Another issue is 'ancient enmities' that linger despite the passage of decades. One such example is Kathy Young, a teen star whose career peaked in 1960, and whose material Ace was keen to license were it not for the producer of the tracks, who fell out with her 45 years ago and still holds a grudge.

Moreover, says Armstrong, some of the licensees, when approached, mistakenly imagine that large amounts of money are in the offing and start to haggle. "When we were doing *A Soldier's Sad Story: Vietnam Through the Eyes of Black America, 1966–1973*, we had one guy who wanted a 'lot more money for this one because of the Iraq war, [because] you'll sell a whole lot more'." Sadly, the artists too can be prone to greed, rather than gratitude, at Ace's overtures.

"Tracking down artists can be a very unrewarding task", says Gibbon, "especially when they come back with unrealistic expectations, enhanced by their lawyers. What we're doing is closer to a public service, no one is going to make fantastic amounts of money." As Carroll adds:

> We want to pay the artists who we license the tracks from fairly, and continue to pay royalties on recordings that are now out of copyright, because there's nothing in any of our contracts that says we stop paying people when British copyright law says it's up. We feel it's morally indefensible to stop payment to people, particularly as they are frequently either very elderly, or if they've died and their families are not wealthy. What the public and most politicians don't realise is, that the £2 or so of royalties that would normally go to the artist and repertoire owner on a regular release, instead goes straight into the pockets of those companies that specialise in releasing CDs of 'out of copyright' recordings.

Another concept that is hard to explain—to some Americans at least—is that of northern soul and the faraway appeal of American artists in improbable parts of the world such as Wigan. "I was going through the records of one label and came across these tapes by a fellow called Lou Roberts", recalls Rudland:

> He had quite a soulful voice. I saw a picture of him, a big trucker with mutton chop whiskers. And I played one of the tracks and it was an okay piece of southern rock, so I passed on that, because Ace isn't about to be putting out southern rock. So, I got back and spoke to Ady [Croasdell] and he says: 'Lou Roberts—he had two massive northern soul hits.' So I was back out there

OPPOSITE CLOCKWISE FROM TOP LEFT:
Richard Berry's *Have "Louie", Will Travel*, 2004; Lou Roberts, circa 1970s; and Richard Berry looking svelte, circa 1960s.

and having to explain to Linda [Lucchesi], the lady who owned the label, the whole concept of the northern soul scene, how these Lou Roberts records were massive in discotheques in the north of England in the late 1970s. It's a really, really weird thing to have to explain to somebody.

However, bootleggers present a far sterner and more serious challenge to legitimate outfits like Ace. As Rudland explains:

> The most frustrating thing about bootleggers is that they don't have to take any time to do their thing. You can spend six months to a year trying to track somebody down and, at any point, the whole deal can be scuppered by some bootlegger putting something out. They always argue: 'Well yeah, how much money do these artists get from you putting out a track on your albums?' Well, sod all maybe. But 'sod all' might be several hundred dollars in the artists' pocket, which is always nice. Or, the fact that their career has been legally restarted means that they can go on to make a hell of a lot of money from the renewed activity and interest in them.

A case in point is Terry Callier, the soul/folk contemporary of Curtis Mayfield who was active in the 1960s but then fell from the scene, only to be

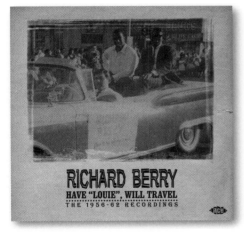

RICHARD BERRY
HAVE "LOUIE", WILL TRAVEL
THE 1956-62 RECORDINGS

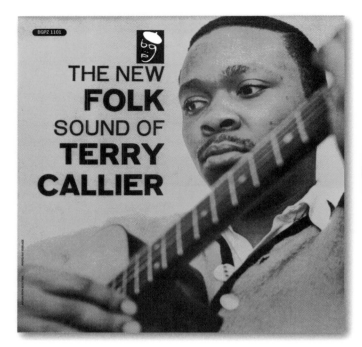

rediscovered in the early 1990s by the acid jazz brigade. "Terry Callier was retired and working as a computer programmer in Chicago before he was tracked down and he's had a huge career since then", says Rudland. "But that whole comeback was very nearly jeopardised by a bootlegger putting out a track of his some three weeks before the proper release. If it had been two months before, the deal might never have happened and Terry wouldn't have had his second career. They do make that kind of difference."

And so, despite the privations, the paper cuts, the mould, the toxic acetate fumes, the crooks, the lawyers, the striplings at record companies and the hard-to-find, sometimes hard-to-persuade beneficiaries of their efforts, Ace persist and, generally, succeed. "Even if it takes several years", says Rounce. "We eventually bring out almost everything we apply for." And, what's more, as Rob Finnis confirms, you just never know what you're going to find:

> We bought the Dore label from Lew Bedell, this indie guy from the late 1950s. He didn't spend too much on records—no strings or orchestras, done fairly basically. Now, he was the guy that discovered Phil Spector. Spector had a huge record with the first record he ever made with The Teddy Bears—"To Know Him, Is To Love Him"—all done for the Dore label for $50. And we have a copy of the original contract, counter-signed by all the group's parents, because the group members were all minors, including Phil Spector (it was signed by his mother, Bertha, who lent her name to Spector's Big Bertha publishing company). Plus, we found an original 78 lacquer of [the same record] in Bedell's garage—a one-off; cut on a lathe—I don't suppose Phil Spector even has a copy. It's gone from LA in the 1950s to a northwest London industrial estate. Anyway, the contract hangs up in Trevor's office. We're all a bit jaded—seen it all, done it all, after a while—but things like that really give you a buzz.

ABOVE LEFT TO RIGHT:

The New Folk Sound of Terry Callier, 2003, and Acetate label for The Teddy Bears' "To Know Him is to Love Him", 1958.

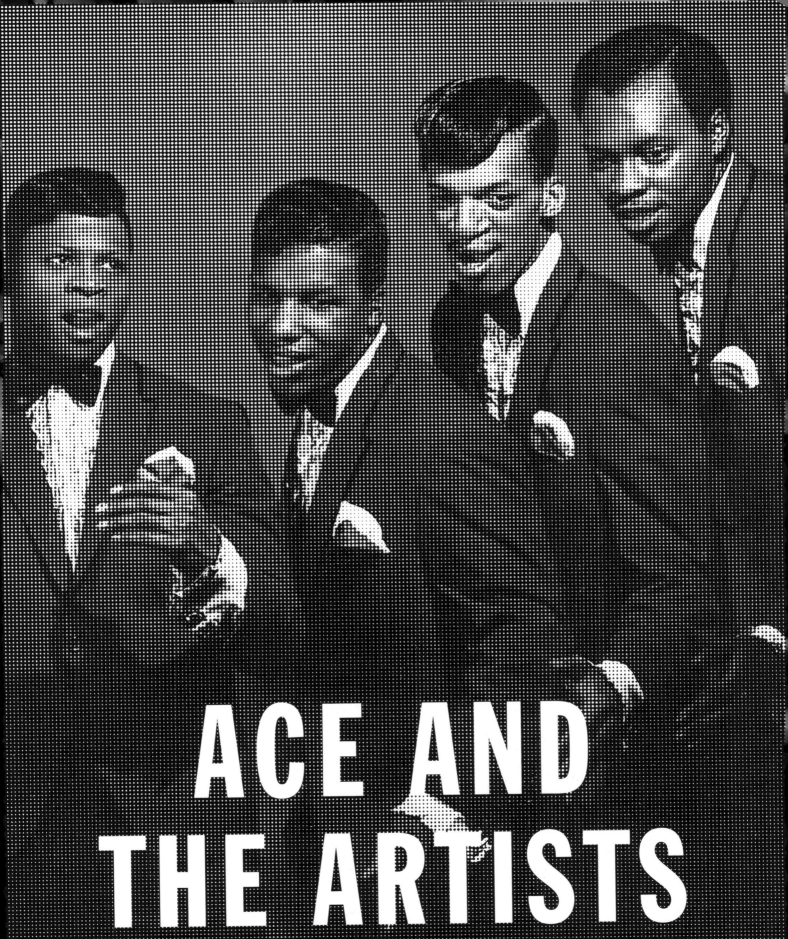

ACE AND THE ARTISTS

Survey Ace's catalogue, or browse through one of the booklets accompanying one of their compilations, and you'll be confronted with a gallery of artists from yesteryear, many of them obscure, many of them featured in the only publicity photos made of them. There is a danger of regarding such artists as iconic but one-dimensional, as signifiers of a lost era—despite the fact that a great many of them are still alive (albeit not always conscious of the esteem in which they are held, if not in their own country, then certainly in Britain and Europe). There is, perhaps, a wish to mentally preserve them—remembering them as they were rather than what they are today. For Ace, however, personal contact with the artist is something they regard as both paramount and one of the more rewarding aspects of the job.

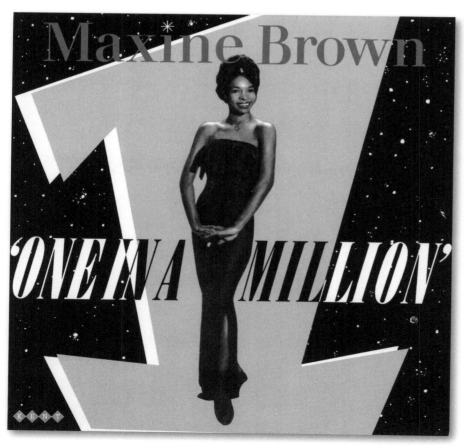

In Association With KENT RECORDS UK

KENT SOUL

Friday 6th June - Sunday 8th June

Present

1997 CLEETHORPES NORTHERN SOUL

ONE IN A MILLION

WEEKENDER

wand

WN 1117 A
(50555)
T.M. Music
Inc., (BMI)
2:59

Prod. by
Steve Tyrell

1650 BROADWAY
NEW YORK, N.Y.

ONE IN A MILLION
(Rudy Clark)
MAXINE BROWN

2 ALL - NIGHTERS
2 ALL DAYERS
AND 3 EVENING SESSIONS

Weekender 97

Record label and photograph courtsey of Paul Temple. Thanks

"They're so keen to talk to you, they're really surprised that you're out there and taking a personal interest in them", says Dean Rudland. "It's amazing how much difference it makes going out there and sitting and talking to them in their homes." With some awe he recalls his own encounters, including a meal with the great Stax artist and songwriter, William Bell:

> We were talking to him at lunch, about cover versions of his stuff and which had been the biggest success. We were thinking of Billy Idol's "To be a Lover" (a mistitled cover of "I Forgot to be Your Lover"), that sold four million. 'That must have been your biggest selling cover, right?' He says: 'Hell, no! Homer Simpson doing "Born Under a Bad Sign"! Five million copies!'

Other Ace consultants have their own memory of first-hand encounters with the artists. Peter Gibbon recalls the exquisite embarrassment of having to croon a song to one of his soul heroines in his own, less than dulcet, tones.

OPPOSITE:
Maxine Brown's *One in a Million*, 1984.

ABOVE:
Poster for 6T's weekender. 1997.
Image courtesy of Ady Croasdell.

"It was at the launch do for the first Stax Box Set", he says. "Carla Thomas was there. I was talking to her and I asked her why a song called "Little Boy" never came out. She said: 'I dunno, how does it go?' So there I was, in front of a singer I've revered all my life, having to sing one of her songs, and I can't carry a note."

Maxine Brown, the versatile soul singer from the 1960s who did not reap anything like the commercial success she deserved, is another of his idols. He, rather gallantly, saved her life when first meeting her in the 1960s. "I interviewed Maxine when she came over in the 1960s, took her out to lunch. [Luckily] I had the presence of mind—when she looked the wrong way while crossing Oxford Street and nearly got mown down by a bus—[to] pull her back." He met her again in the early 1990s in New York. Reminding her that he had rescued her from a collision with a London bus back in 1966, he tried to persuade her to come to Britain and perform—at the 100 Club, and Cleethorpes. He assured her that it wouldn't be the same as her previous visit (when she had been accommodated in poor quality, back street hotels due to lack of budget, on the promoter's behalf, and because British hoteliers of the period hadn't been keen on black artists). Brown was eventually persuaded and has since been a regular visitor to Britain, culminating in her headline act at Kent's twenty-fifth anniversary show in 2007. As Tony Rounce says:

> Sometimes it's not the artists but their children with whom Ace end up dealing, and who are often astonished at the legacy they have been bequeathed. I occasionally get emails or letters from the sons or daughters of some of the artists we deal with saying, 'thanks to your work I've come to know a lot more about my father or mother than I was ever able to find out before', because their records weren't available.

Of course, of equal value for money are the people who run the independent labels themselves who, by necessity, would have had to be pretty durable characters in their different ways in order to set up such establishments in America in the 1950s and 60s. Ady Croasdell recalls his encounter with one of them:

> There's a label called Carnival Records in New Jersey—the owner is Joe Evans, a sweet old guy who picked me up from a snowbound Newark Airport. As I got to know him more, I realised he had quite a musical history: he was a brilliant saxophonist, he'd played with Charlie Parker, Dizzy Gillespie, been on the first

OPPOSITE:
Flyer for Kent's 25th Anniversary show at The Forum, 19 October 2007.

BELOW LEFT TO RIGHT:
Carnival artists, The Cymbals and *The Mariachi Brass*, a musical genre that experienced renewed popularity after this Ace release.

SHOW & DANCE

THE FORUM

9-17 Highgate Rd, Kentish Town, **LONDON** - NW5 1JY

FRIDAY NITE OCT. 19 2007

ADMISSION: £22
7:30PM - 2AM

TICKET DETAILS WWW.SEETICKETS.COM (0870-150-0044)   WWW.ACERECORDS.COM   WWW.6TS.INFO

KENT RECORDS

1982-2007
25 YEAR ANNIVERSARY

ALL IN PERSON!

"WHERE THE HITS LIVE FOREVER!"

"NOTHING BUT A HEARTACHE"

MAXINE BROWN

"OH NO, NOT MY BABY"

the FLIRTATIONS

TOMMY HUNT

"LOVING ON THE LOSING SIDE"

Mary LOVE

"LAY THIS BURDEN DOWN"

WINFIELD PARKER

"28 DAYS"
"I'M WONDERIN"

KENT SOUL

ALL IN PERSON!

PLUS *original* 6TS *djs* IAN CLARK, MICK SMITH & ADY CROASDELL   *SPINNING TO A GREAT DANCEFLOOR!*

Parking is restricted in Kentish Town, please use public transport: Kentish Town British Rail, Underground & Buses 134, 214 & C2, car parking available in Regis Road, NW5.

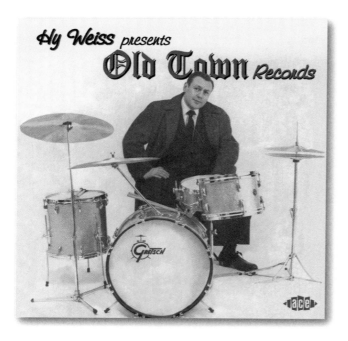

Motown reviews, played at the Savoy, Apollo, at the height of the jitterbug reviews, playing with 'Slide' Hampton, Louis Armstrong—been there, done it all. Later on in life, after he retired to Richmond, Virginia, he decided to go to an evening class to learn about the history of jazz. There was a young lecturer teaching him and, after a few weeks, Joe said 'actually, I've had a bit of a career in music myself' and gave him copies of the CDs we'd done which include sleeve notes describing Joe's life. At the next class, the lecturer says: 'You know, I feel like such an idiot standing up here. There's a guy here who knows more, who's done more in jazz than I'll ever do. I should be sitting out there with you, listening to him!' And he ended up writing a book on Joe's life.

'Sweet', by contrast, is not a characteristic that springs immediately to mind in the case of recently deceased Hy Weiss—the wily, old school operator with whom Ace cut a deal to handle some of the blues, pop and R&B on his roster, including acts Sonny Terry, Brownie McGee and Billy Bland. As Gibbon recalls:

There are legendary stories about (Weiss) and his cohorts. He was having a business discussion that wasn't going well and, the legend goes, he hung the guy out of the window by his ankles—whereupon the guy signed the contract. In later years, I worked up the courage to ask him if this story was true. He chuckled and said: 'Sure it was, but what they never tell you in that story is that it was a basement window!'

Armstrong and Weiss became firm friends over the years when Ace licensed his Old Town label. He always stayed at Weiss' home when he was in the New York area. "You could learn a lot from a man like that", says Armstrong.

ABOVE:

Hy Weiss Presents Old Town Records, 2003.

"A CHANGE IS GONNA COME"

In 2003, Ace consultant Tony Rounce put together a compilation which brought to the fore a more socially and politically conscious strain—both on Ace's part and that of 1960s American soul music. Rounce was intrigued that, despite the antiwar movement in Vietnam being largely perceived as a white, hippy, middle class liberal affair, it was given surprisingly short shrift in white 1960s rock music: "There were only about eight or nine white rock records, really, back in the 1960s, which really addressed Vietnam. You've got Country Joe and Creedence Clearwater Revival, then you really are beginning to struggle. But in soul, you've got so many of them. And soul fans have always talked about those records."

The simple reason for that, believes Rounce is that, alongside 'poor white trash', hillbillies and the like, it was young, black Americans who were being sent out to fight the war—while, in the main, middle class liberals got to stay at home and be concerned in safety. For black people, the war was very much more a reality. "This was especially the case once they shifted the qualifications you needed in order to be enlisted", says Rounce. "And that's why the two genres of music that have the most number of Vietnam War records are soul and country."

Hence *A Soldier's Sad Story: Vietnam Through The Eyes of Black America, 1966–1973*, which tracks the progress of soul's response to the conflict through its recordings. Early on, these are not so much agit-pop in tone but, rather, express the distress of the prospect of having to leave loved ones behind. Any protest in The Monitors' "Greetings (This is Uncle Sam)" or William Bell's "Marching off to War" is either coded or muted. However, as the War begins to take its toll, the tone of these songs—although more personal than political—begins to darken, as is evident in releases such as Emmanuel Lasky's "Letter From Vietnam". Gradually, artists such as Freda "Band of Gold" Payne and Edwin Starr laid populism on the line with the explicit "Bring our Boys Home" and "Stop the War Now" respectively. However, it is the recordings of the early 1970s, as the Vietnam War was winding down, which are the most telling. Singles like Curtis Mayfield's "Back to the World" and Bill Withers' haunting "I Can't Write Left Handed" would begin to reflect the trauma and aftermath of those black conscripts who, on returning home, found they still had to fight the same battles on the domestic front.

James Maycock's liner notes offer a vivid, historical and anecdotal backdrop to all of this, drawing on the oral history of black troops who mock Hollywood depictions of white American troops finger popping to black records. "That's

ACE RECORDS

OPPOSITE CLOCKWISE FROM TOP LEFT:
Change is Gonna Come—The Voice of Black America 1964–1973, 2007; poster for Country Joes and The Fish's "I Feel Like I'm Fixin' to Die"; and *A Soldier's Sad Story—Vietnam Through the Eyes of Black America 1966–1973*, 2003.

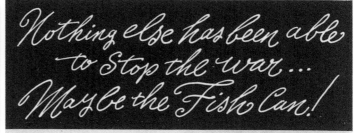

revisionism", says one. In fact, there were attempts to withdraw soul music from the jukeboxes and the Armed Forces Radio Network played mostly country.

2007 then saw another Rounce-compiled release, *Change Is Gonna Come: The Voice of Black America 1963–1973*, which tracks the slow 'unmasking' of American soul music as the Civil Rights Movement gathered pace in the 1960s. Rounce, as a young white Briton, found himself exposed to images of pacifist black protestors being hosed down by the National Guard, and to television coverage of the aftermath of Martin Luther King's assignation. As a young soul fanatic, the sense of injustice all this engendered in him only served to bolster his empathy with the music he loved. And so, from Otis Redding's exquisitely cut cover of Sam Cooke's "A Change is Gonna Come", we progress through the increasingly strident likes of The Staple Singers' *When Will We Be Paid?*. A musical journey like this could not but end with the inevitable "The Revolution Will Not Be Televised" by Gil Scott-Heron. Along the way, Rounce picks some strange fruit, not least actor (and Bond villain) Yaphet Kotto's pre-rap oratory, "Have You Ever Seen The Blues".

"In recent years, we haven't developed new labels or promoted new genres, but what we have developed is these series and ideas, like *The Golden Age of American Rock'n'Roll*", says Roger Armstrong:

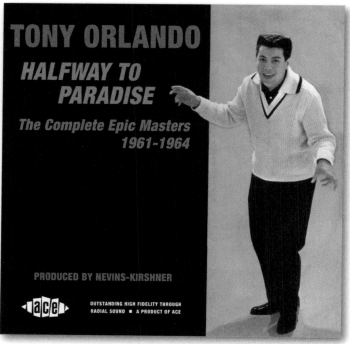

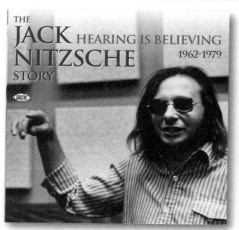

The producer/writer series, the Jack Nitzsche volumes, the *Change is Gonna Come* compilation about the American Civil Rights Movement, the Vietnam CDs—all of that has taken the idea of the reissue to such a remove from when we first started out. What's evolved is the breadth and depth of knowledge, the first hand research we've done, and these series have taken the idea of the reissue into the realms of full-blown publishing. I say we don't just put out records, we publish. You get the music, you get the packaging, you get the photos, you get the notes, the stories.

Peruse Ace's catalogue today and you will find, to take but a small sample, works by Roy Acuff, the baseball player turned 'king of country music', country soul Leviathan Arthur Alexander, one-man break beat trove David Axelrod, Joan Baez, The Bambi Molesters ('Croatia's number one surf band'), acoustic guitar adventurist Robbie Basho, Chuck Berry, James Carr and gospel legend Sister Wynona Carr, Caucasian all-girl 1950s harmony quartet The Chordettes, Sam Cooke and The Soul Stirrers, the Woodstock-defining Country Joe & The Fish, Fats Domino, John Fahey, the late acoustic fingerpicker who ranged from ultra traditional to avant-garde, the late Mimi (sister of Joan Baez) and the late Richard Farina, Funk Inc, John Hammond, Loleatta Holloway, The Holy Modal Rounders, Lightnin' Hopkins, The Ikettes, Wanda Jackson, the 'Queen of Rockabilly' ("That was sheer luck. We applied to EMI for a compilation of Wanda Jackson's rockabilly sides—and remarkably it cleared," says Armstrong of Ace's *Queen of Rockabilly* CD), Albert King, The Latin Jazz Quintet, Stirling Moss (a recording of a 1958 interview with the British Grand Prix driver), Macedonian saxophonist Ferus Mustafov, Ohio Players, Tony Orlando (who was so pleased with the job Ace did on reissuing his early work, he asked the label if they could supply him with copies to sell at the 300 or so concerts he currently performs annually—the nature of the deal Ace had struck with Sony/BMG meant that they had to decline), Chuck Rio, 'The Tequila Man', Buffy Sainte-Marie, Joe Simon, Sly Stone (his early work, 1963–1965), Strawberry Alarm Clock, Big Mama Thornton (the Blues shouter who recorded the original "Hound Dog"), 3 Pieces, the Donald Byrd-produced combo, Canadian singer-songwriter Ian Tyson, The Fabulous Wailers (the Seattle rock'n'rollers, not the Bob Marley variety), Larry Williams and Young Jessie. No narrative, if it has any chance of being remotely linear, can hope to embrace such far-flung diversity.

Today, Ace operates from Tardis-like premises nestled discreetly next to a canal, on the edge of an industrial estate on northwest London. However, as well as providing offices for the Ace staff, the building also contains a large warehouse area, and extensive cleaning up and studio facilities. Shelves and entire rooms are filled with books, files, computers, relics of old studio equipment, sound files, tapes, CDs and masters.

A constant feature at Ace has been the sound quality of their CDs, which is largely due to the remarkable skills of the engineers at Sound Mastering Ltd (SML), the post-production studio subsidiary of Ace. Originally set up by Adam Skeaping in his own home he, and his then *protégé* Duncan Cowell, later moved to the Ace building where acoustically-treated rooms were custom built at a fairly hefty expense. First, Bob Jones brought his knowledge of rock'n'roll sound to the team. Later, Nick Robbins—who had worked with Armstrong as a recording engineer at Elephant Studio—began work at the studio.

Cowell's work on the *Golden Age of American Rock'n'Roll* series has come in for considerable praise and rightfully so. In tandem with Churchill's sourcing

OPPOSITE CLOCKWISE FROM TOP LEFT:
The Latin Jazz Quintet's *Latin Soul*, 1994; Tony Orlando's *Halfway to Paradise*, 2006; David Axelrod's *Heavy Axe*, 1998; Wanda Jackson's *Queen of Rockabilly*, 2000; Chuck Berry's *On the Blues Side*, 1993; Joan Baez's *Joan Baez*, circa 2000; *Hearing is Believing–The Jack Nitzsche Story: Vol 1*, 2005; and *Hard Workin' Man–The Jack Nitzsche Story: Vol 2*, 2006.

ACE RECORDS

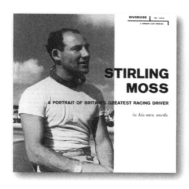

of the best possible audio, Cowell's general finesse in his approach to sound engineering has harvested spectacular results.

"Our job is to make the finished listening experience such that the listener is unaware of the work that has gone into the post-production", says Cowell: "It should be seamless, with all the tracks sounding like they are part of the same record, even when it's an artists compilation of 24 very different recordings." Robbins points out that, "with the advances in digital technology over the last few years, we can now get to grips with the audio in a way that was not possible even 10 years ago". Though he spent many years working on multitrack tapes in the recording studio, he says: "Both Duncan and I love to work from the original 16" acetates of the late 1940s and early 50s. The sound is so rich, open and very responsive." This combination of traditional recording means and materials, along with twenty-first century digital technology, produces the pristine sound that Ace has become rightfully renowned for.

"Fortunately, most of the vital stuff is held in fireproof archives", says Gibbon:

> Also, much of the stuff is on digital servers and backed up. Only a few years ago, [because of the] the scale of what we're doing, you'd have to be in the realms of the CIA in order to store all our data. We used to have multiple copies of things on DAT. It's not like the old days. I know of a collector of 78s—his house caught fire and burned for 36 hours, even with the fire brigade there—all that shellac.

Walk around the Ace headquarters and you might discover a pile of unopened cardboard boxes, cargo from some recent American label acquisition waiting for Gibbon to start forensic work on—only to turn left and find yourself in a state-of-the-art mastering suite. This being Ace, they also require top of the range equipment to clean up the many acetates and discs they acquire. "We have this huge, Heath Robinson-type record cleaning machine", says Gibbon. "The guys that came along with that said: 'We have the Library of Congress and the BBC as customers—we'd like to have you.' Roger left the room—I thought he was leaving in disgust but he'd gone to get the cheque book."

Such acquisitions serve to aid the compilation of an amazingly comprehensive and detailed profile of the music of an era which, given the more flexible conditions of modern day recording, allows for a more complete picture than could be possible for contemporary music. "I thought, in the 1960s, that we'd never be able to document 1960s music", says Gibbon. "Now, 1960s music is the most documented in our database, the 1970s less so, the 1980s and 90s, who knows?"

OPPOSITE:
James Carr, circa 1960s—Goldwax recording artist and one of the word's greatest soul singers.
Image courtesy of Quinton Claunch.

ABOVE LEFT TO RIGHT:
 A Portrait of Britain's Greatest Racing Driver, 2003,—the autobiography of Stirling Moss. Moss personally visited the Ace offices to buy copies of the CD— much to the delight of the label's sales manager and F1 fanatic, Phil Stoker; Sly Stone's *Precious Stone*, 1994; Big Mama Thornton's *Jail*, 1995; and The Fabulous Wailers' *At The Castle/& Company*, 2003.

One of the key aspects of the publishing work Ace do for each sleeve is the artwork. Being a reissues label, one might assume that all Ace do is appropriate the sleeve designs of yesteryear—with all the era's evocations of a smarter, classier, more immaculate age—and simply reduce them to CD size. This is simply not the way it happens. Since many of Ace's releases are compilations of singles by artists who, in many cases, did not release an album of their own, they must produce an original sleeve concept. This must be evocative of the age but, as Carol Fawcett (who is responsible for commissioning much of Ace's artwork) insists: "We don't do pastiche." Moreover, she abhors much of the visual treatment meted out to recording artists in the 1950s and 60s, which was not as carefully conceived and executed as is often imagined. A crude cut out of Marvin Gaye's head superimposed on Superman's body, is a case in point. As for black artists, there was often reluctance to feature them on cover sleeves at all, preferring, for example, images of sultry white females in order to reach a crossover market.

Ace's early design brief was, as Fawcett wrote for the notes accompanying an exhibition of Ace design at the Art Vinyl Gallery in Broadway Market, London, in 2006, to "capture the essence of the period and style of music, without it pretending to be an exact copy of the past". Most adept at this was Phil Smee of Waldo's Design, one of the first designers employed during the Chiswick era, and still used for the most prestigious of Ace's projects. He would work up ideas generated from Ted Carroll's extensive collection of 1950s LPs, designed in the pre-Letraset era, to produce something in line with Ace's philosophy as a whole. The visual world of Ace, then, is not so much idealised as idealistic.

There is idealism too, albeit hand in hand with commercialism, in the way they conduct business—be it with their own staff, paying suppliers or in their treatment of artists. In 2005, Jon King of Gang of Four was asked why someone like him, who specialised in acerbic critiques of capitalism, should have signed

to a major label back in the late 1970s. King replied cynically, that in his experience, the crop of indie labels that emerged during and after punk were run by shysters and, given the choice, he preferred working in the context of 'late' Capitalism (ie. the well-developed corporate labels, rather than the 'early' Capitalist, liable-to-be-crooked indies).

This is certainly a valid critique in part—being an independent label did not necessarily entail a lack of sharp practice or of ripping off artists. However, neither Chiswick nor Ace belong in this category by any means. Churchill, Armstrong and Carroll have undoubtedly done well for themselves over the years but they have always been determined to treat their artists fairly, as Nick Garrard, manager of The Meteors, points out:

We had a contract with Chiswick whereby if the distributor doesn't pay them, they don't have to pay the artist royalties on records they hadn't been paid for. But when Pinnacle, the distributor, went bust, they made a decision to pay all royalties anyway, which I thought was extremely fair. At the end of the day, Ted, Roger and Trevor are as much fans of the music and the musicians as they are interested in making money. I can't imagine any other company doing that. They're dead straight. Every year, my royalty cheques always arrive on time, without fail.

Armstrong and Carroll have campaigned vocally against laws regarding copyright lapse, seeing the effect it would have on some of the financially poorer and elderly musicians with whom they deal. Churchill, meanwhile, is lobbying for a practical, central licensing database available to all, which would put an end to the more cumbersome, case by case system still in use today. As for the future, there is still no end to the archaeological digging in sight, although Gibbon believes that one or two genres, such as doo-wop, have had their heyday in terms of the material still to be discovered.

The arrival of the Internet has altered the realities of trading. These days, it's no longer about racks in record stores, as there are fewer record stores. As things transfer online, however, international markets such as America, and Japan (where there is a huge collecting scene) can shop more conveniently. So much for the days of market stalls, wheeler dealing, jumble sale swapsies and fingering through stacks of antique vinyl. However, as Phil Stoker, Ace's sales director confirms, most consumers of Ace's collection essentially want three things: the music quality (which downloads still can't provide); the in-depth sleeve notes and illustrated package and lastly the compilation itself. It is often the concept that a purchaser wants—rather than a random collection of tracks—a skillful compilation with a linking narrative that tells both a literary and musical story.

And yet, as music genres increasingly become atemporal, there is a healthy future in the past. Nick Garrard cites the example of a young, rockabilly group, Kitty, Daisy and Lewis. "They collect American 78s—and two of them are still at school. Dad plays piano; Mum plays double bass and then three of the most gorgeous kids you can imagine—quite a Brady Bunch vibe!"

They're not alone. A few weekends ago, a friend and I rounded off a birthday party by staggering into an after-hours establishment in east London. During regular hours it was a strip joint but after 11pm it converts into a bar, a magnificent, gaudy throwback to the vintage era of the late 1950s, with revellers decades younger than myself snappily attired and lacquered back in the styles popular in the decade before I was born, dancing the night away to a vinyl soundtrack of rockabilly, girl groups, rock'n'roll. When I staggered out at 4.30 am, the joint was still jumping, the place still packed. Backwards, forwards, it goes on and on....

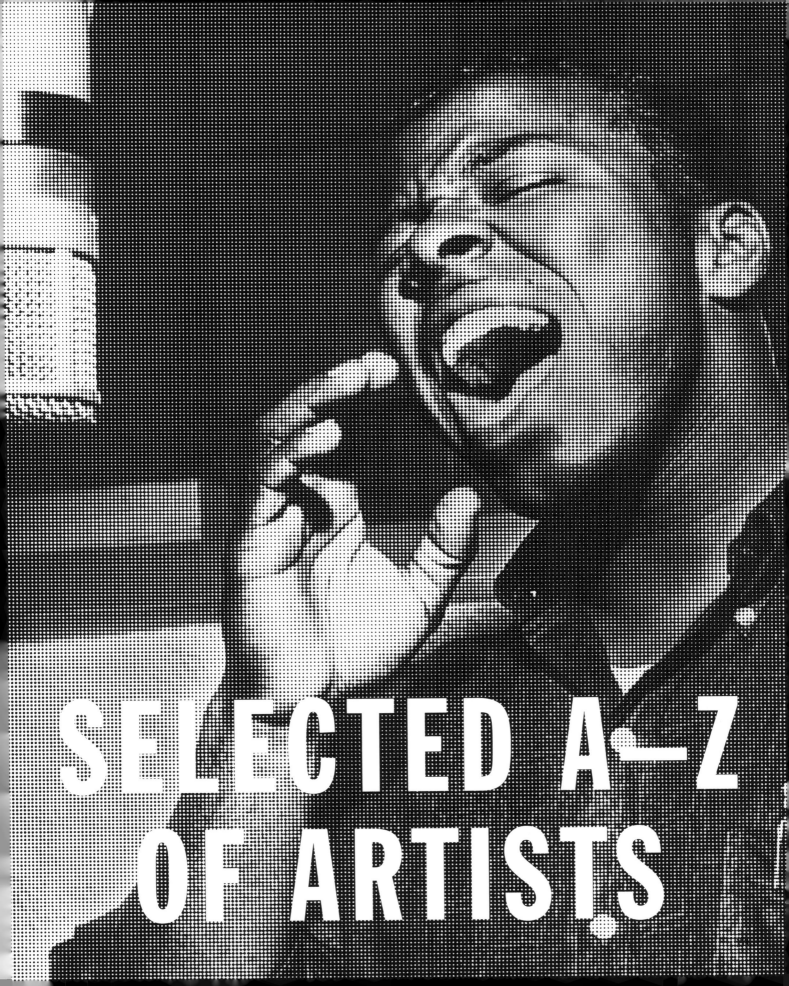

SELECTED A–Z
OF ARTISTS

SELECTED A–Z OF ARTISTS

Code: (TC) Ted Carroll, (RA) Roger Armstrong, (AP) Alec Palao, (TR) Tony Rounce, (AC) Ady Croasdell, (DR) Dean Rudland, (RF) Rob Finnis.

3 MUSTAPHAS 3

In 1985, from Szegerely's Crazy Loquat Bar, came 3 Mustaphas 3; plucking, banging, sawing and blowing strange instruments unknown to a wary EEC (European Economic Community) public. Before too long, however, they won the public's hearts, made frequent appearances on television and engaged audiences in their very unique stories and songs. They made three and two half LPs in five hectic years and toured the world with good humour, great music and stunning head wear. (RA)

ARTHUR ALEXANDER

Arthur Alexander, born in Florence, Alabama, on 10 May 1940, was one of the greatest country soul singers ever. His influence was immense and he inspired countless singers and musicians. His fans included the Beatles, the Rolling Stones, Bob Dylan, Dusty Springfield, the Bee Gees, Ike & Tina Turner and Ry Cooder, all of whom made cover versions of his records.

Alexander's first record "Sally Sue Brown"—released on the Judd label in 1960 as "Junie Alexander"—had picked up some airplay, so Rick Hall took him to his newly built FAME studio in Muscle Shoals to record a follow up. He cut another of the Alexander's songs "You Better Move On" which was released on the Dot label and made it to number 24 on the billboard chart in 1962. A string of classic recordings followed, including "Anna", "Soldiers of Love", "Where Have You Been", "A Shot of Rhythm & Blues" and "You're the Reason". Although several of his best-known recordings were his own compositions, Alexander was also a masterful interpreter of others' songs.

His unique singing style was very precise, but laid back, and the timbre of his voice added to the emotion and poignancy he invested in every recording.

In later years, Alexander drifted into obscurity and spent many years working as a bus driver. Ace's reissue of his classic early recordings did much to focus on his wonderful talent and, eventually, he was persuaded to start performing again. Sadly, in 1993—just three days after performing in Nashville with his new band and after recording a new album—he died of a heart attack. (TC)

JOAN BAEZ

With a voice so pure that it barely seems possible, Joan Baez has soared over the folk scene through five decades. She cut countless albums for Vanguard, mixing traditional songs with releases by the very best of her contemporaries. Among these was Bob Dylan, whose music she interpreted in a way that complemented his own reading perfectly, and that framed his melodies in a quite magnificent way. She made country records with Nashville's finest, sang with Kris Kristofferson, had various members of the Grateful Dead accompanying her and, of course, produced those memorable duets with Dylan at Newport. (RA)

HANK BALLARD

John Henry Kendricks, aka Hank Ballard, was born in Detroit on 18 November 1936. He first started singing in his local church and, later, sang with a few local groups before joining the Royals in 1953 (at Johnny Otis' instigation) and singing lead on the Otis-penned "Every Beat of My Heart".

Later that year, the Royals made number six on the R&B chart with "Get It", the first of which was to become a string of laviscious hits penned by Ballard. The following year, the group were forced to change their name when the better-known 5 Royals joined the same label (Federal). The group's first release as Hank Ballard & The Midnighters, "Work With Me Annie", reached number one on the R&B chart and number 22 in the pop charts, and they found further success that year with "Sexy Ways" and "Annie Had A Baby".

By 1959, the group had switched to the King label and scored a number four hit in the R&B chart with the great "Teardrops On Your Letter". However, it was the B-side of this release—another Ballard composition—"The Twist" which was to be the major influence on the rest of his career. "The Twist" was covered by Chubby Checker, a young singer who scored a number one pop hit with it for the Philly-based Cameo Parkway label. Checker went onto launch the twist craze with a number of other twist records, while Ballard continued to sell well into the 1960s with a string of dance hits, including "Finger Poppin' Time", "Let's Go, Let's Go, Let's Go", "The Switch-A-Roo", "The Continental Walk" and "The Float".

Failing to adapt successfully to the changing tastes of 1970s record buyers, Ballard worked the oldies circuit and enjoyed a comfortable lifestyle courtesy of a healthy royalty stream from his song writing hits. He died of cancer at the age of 66 at his Los Angeles home on 2 March 2003—living long enough to be inducted into the Rock'n'Roll Hall of Fame in 1990. (TC)

CHIEF DR SIKURU AYINDE BARRISTER

Chief Dr Sikuru Ayinde Barrister (aka Barry Wonder) is synonymous with the explosive percussive sound of Fuji (based on Islamic music, but with roots that trace back into Nigeria's past). Born in 1948, he joined the army in 1967—during Nigeria's Civil War—where he started his musical career. He left the army in 1976 and became a full time musician—going from strength to strength with his four singers, ten percussionists and a Hawaiian steel guitar (often playing seven hour sets at a time). He has made countless recordings, with his GlobeStyle Records outing *New Fuji Garbage* particularly championed. (RA)

WILLIAM BELL

Singer, writer, producer and all round good-guy, William Bell, was with Stax from the early days and stayed with the label until 1974. He debuted on Stax with "You Don't Miss Your Water", which subsequently became a classic, spawning countless covers. His understated style contrasted with the more sanctified vocals of many of his contemporaries and much of his success was with ballads like "I Forgot To Be Your Lover". One notable exception was, of course, the smash duet with Judy Clay on "Private Number" that proved he could handle 'sanctified' soul with the best of them. The CD of out-takes from *A Little Something Extra* also shows that he could handle a broad range of material from the beginning. (RA)

RICHARD BERRY

Richard Berry was born on 11 April 1935 in Extension, Louisiana. When still a child, he moved with his family to LA in search of a better life. A natural musician, his first musical adventure was learning to play ukulele at summer camp. By his mid-teens (while still at high school), he was singing and recording with numerous vocal groups in South LA.

If Richard Berry's only contribution to music was to write and record "Louie Louie", one of the most popular and most performed songs in pop, this would put him head and shoulders above most of his contemporaries. However, some of Berry's other career highlights include: lead vocal on the classic "Riot in Cell Block Number Nine" by the Robins; singing the male counterpart to Etta James on her hit "Wallflower" (which he also produced) and recording/writing the classic "Have Love Will Travel", which became a huge hit for the Sonics. He was a prolific writer and producer and sang with countless LA groups, notably the Flairs and the Chimes, as well as his own groups, the Pharaohs and the Dreamers. Before his death, on 23 January 1997 at his home in Los Angeles, Berry was able to enjoy the fame and financial benefits from his best known song writing copyrights. (TC)

BOBBY BLAND

More than 55 years after he stopped being Junior Parker's chauffeur (and started to make some of the most amazing examples of black American music that the world will ever hear) Bobby 'Blue' Bland remains at the top of his game. The recordings that he made during his two decades as Duke Records' flagship artist shaped the future strand of R&B that would become known as 'blue soul', and his influence on a range of equally important artists that include Little Milton, Dan Penn and Van Morrison can never be overstated. (TR)

BOOKER T & THE MG'S

Booker T & The MG's have probably played on more hits than any band on the planet. As the Stax house band they accompanied nearly every singer on the label up until the 1970s. They issued over 11 albums of their own on Stax and scored 14 R&B hits. In addition to these statistics, is a group of musicians with an insightful understanding of mood and tempo and an uncanny ability to shift the focus of a piece—as the instruments weave in and out of each other. No other group has quite achieved this in the same way, though they have been flattered with countless imitations. (RA)

HADDA BROOKS

The former Hadda Hopgood was the 'First Lady' of Modern Records—quite literally, as she was the first artist to appear on the R&B imprint. A serious pianist who was first cajoled into playing boogie woogie, and then singing (by Modern's boss Jules Bihari), her 78s—especially those which featured her intimate, beguiling vocal purr—played a major part in shaping the sound of post-war West Coast R&B.

Brooks' profile began to slowly dwindle after she left Modern, and her contributions to the genesis of R&B were largely overlooked for many years. However, her happy rediscovery in the 1990s, supplemented by new recordings that she made for Virgin/Pointblank, and an ongoing series of CD reissues from Ace (which feature many previously unissued and undocumented Modern recordings), ensured that her career ended on the same high with which it started in 1944's "Swinging the Boogie". (TR)

MAXINE BROWN

Maxine Brown has been singing soul since its very inception. The late music journalist and soul guru, Dave Godin, considered her self-penned hit "All In My Mind" to be one of the very first soul records and a pinnacle of deep soul artistry.

Brown's most prolific and best-loved work was recorded for New York's Wand label and included the original (and best) version of Goffin and King's soul anthem "Oh No Not My Baby", a big hit for Manfred Mann. While at Wand, Brown cut a string of sublime 1960s soul dance tracks that have been adopted by the British northern soul crowd. These include "One in a Million", "Let Me Give You My Loving", "One Step at a Time" and "It's Torture".

She continued to record through the 1960s and 70s for Sony's Epic label and Commonwealth United records, but it was not until an appearance at the legendary Cleethorpes Northern Soul Weekender in the 1990s that she revived her career and now sings to sell-out crowds around Europe and the USA. (AC)

TERRY CALLIER

When Terry Callier retired from the music business in 1982, he turned his back on nearly 20 years of recording that never quite saw him make a breakthrough. However, just eight years later, he was reclaimed by London's soul and acid jazz scenes to become a surprise success, with a major label deal, sell-out dates at large theatres, reappraisal of his catalogue and recognition as the musical genius that he truly was. This was partly the result of his first album being reissued on Beat Goes Public—the delicately beautiful folk blues of *New Folk Sound*—which had been recorded using two bass players (because that was how John Coltrane played). (DR)

JAMES CARR

James Carr's original 1967 recording of Dan Penn and Chips Moman's "The Dark End of the Street" defines southern and deep soul in a way that few other records have done. Ace has issued, across five CDs, every recording that the late, and truly great, Carr ever made. The consistency of his 1960s recordings for Memphis' Goldwax label will always be at odds with the relentless torment and tragedy of his personal circumstances, but such was his talent that he could leave his problems at the studio door and deliver definitive versions of any song, on any given session. Carr's psychological problems kept him away from the recording scene for too many of his peak years, but he came back strong in the early 1990s—after an almost 15 year absence—with new recordings; showing a true soul fire can never be extinguished. (TR)

THE CHAMPS AND CHUCK RIO

The Champs were one of the greatest instrumental bands of the rock'n'roll era. The group evolved from the musical partnership between guitarist, Dave Burgess, and saxophone player, Danny Flores (aka Chuck Rio). The two had been gigging around the clubs of Los Angeles as Danny & Dave, backed by Rio's band.

Burgess was signed as a vocalist to Challenge, a small LA-based label co-owned by singing cowboy, Gene Autry. In mid-1957, Danny & Dave recorded an instrumental to try to emulate the popularity of the smash hit "Raunchy". The single, recorded at Goldstar studios in Hollywood, was the wonderfully atmospheric "Train To Nowhere". They recorded a throwaway instrumental, "Tequila", as a B-side.

Re-released by the Champs (with whom Flores assumed the identity of 'Chuck Rio' as he was already signed to another label) the record was a number one hit within three weeks, and "Tequila" was moved to the A-side. The band recorded several more great instrumental releases, including "El Rancho Rock" and "Midnighter", before Rio left after an argument with Burgess. The band continued touring and recording with Burgess at the helm. Many, now famous, musicians passed through their ranks, including Jimmy Seals & Dash Crofts, Johnny Meeks, Glenn Campbell and Jerry Cole.

The Champs continued recording and touring until 1965, when—on Burgess' instigation—the group wound up. Rio, known as the Godfather of Latino Rock, was a tremendous live performer and great tenor player and continued touring and recording until shortly before his death in 2006. (TC)

CHOCOLATE WATCHBAND

Bursting out of the San Francisco Bay Area in early 1966—with a ferocious stage act of exaggerated British R&B—the Chocolate Watchband were the quintessential psychedelic garage band bar none, as punky singles like "Sweet Young Thing" attest. Signed by LA producer, Ed Cobb, the group watched haplessly as their studio efforts were hacked to pieces, only to resurface on instant tax-loss albums that clogged the racks in discount stores. Ironically, these same cut-outs—along with enticing glimpses in films like *Riot On Sunset Strip*—would prompt collector interest in the Chocolate Watchband long after their demise, and lead indirectly to the group's immense cult reputation today. (AP)

THE COUNT BISHOPS

The Count Bishops were formed in the summer of 1975 when guitarist Zenon Hieroski left his previous band, Chrome, and joined forces with singer Mike Spenser, who had just arrived from New York. After placing an advertisement in *Melody Maker* Australian drummer, Paul Balbi, and bass player, Stevie Lewins, joined the band. The Count Bishops were complete when Spenser's friend, guitarist Johnny Guitar, came on board.

On 28 August 1975 they cut their first record with Chiswick, a four track EP entitled *Speedball*, in the tiny Pathway studio with Roger Armstrong. Chiswick then signed the band (minus Spenser, with whom the band had parted ways) to an exclusive deal. Just before they went into Jackson's

Studio to record an album with engineer, Vic Maile, they were joined by vocalist Dave Tice. The subsequent album, *The Bishops,* had considerable airplay from John Peel and Kid Jensen and sold well for a virtually unknown band.

In March 1979 Hieroski died in a car accident. A second studio album, *Crosscuts*, had been completed before his death and so the band decided to carry on. It was released in May but a month later, on returning from a tour of Spain, Paul Balbi was detained by British immigration and deported back to Australia. The loss of two key members spelt the end of the group and they eventually split at the end of 1979. 26 years later, the original line reformed to play Ace Records Thirtieth Birthday Bash (in London in 2005) with a large blow-up photo of Hieroski as a stage backdrop. (TC)

COUNT FIVE

In the summer of 1966, "Psychotic Reaction"—the masterpiece of teenaged angst that sauntered into the national Top 10—was being blasted out from transistor radios all across America. Sporting the same disaffected cool as the Stones and Yardbirds, Count Five embodied the quintessential suburban punk achievement: one solid stone hit and then straight back to nowhere. In fact, the group had such an uneventful subsequent career that gonzo rock writer Lester Bangs famously invented one for them. Yet, in a mere two-and-a-half minutes "Psychotic Reaction" perfectly articulated—in sound and fury—the frustration of youthful America in those heady days. (AP)

COUNTRY JOE & THE FISH

Country Joe & The Fish's 1967 debut LP, *Electric Music For The Mind & Body*, was the defining moment at which the attitude and philosophies of the emergent rock counter-culture were matched by what was in the grooves. The group was born amid the folk-fuelled turbulence of Berkeley but, while the humour of classics such as the Woodstock "I Feel Like I'm Fixin' to Die" branded singer Country Joe MacDonald a rancorous politico, it was the group's musical acid visions that truly struck a chord, making them the first Bay Area group that could legitimately be called 'psychedelic'. (AP)

THE CRAMPS

The most exalted potentates of rock'n'roll have been distilling the shimmy and the shake since 1976, mutating its second cousin, rockabilly, in a familial cross-breeding of surf and psyche to produce a musical monster that frightened the life into Frank N Stein. Add to this Film Noir and Horror, and late night TV, and you have the incredible phenomena that are The Cramps. Ivy Rorschach (big shimmering guitar) and Lux Interior (big loud vocals) populate Crampsville, a place where few have dared to tread. (RA)

THE DAMNED

From the first thrilling rush of punk rock with "New Rose" in 1976, The Damned set themselves apart from the politico posturing of most of their contemporaries. They were politically incorrect and perfectly proud of the fact. They were concerned with chaos and carnage and were by far the best band in town—the ultimate 'no no' for the punk fashionistas. They went from strength to strength cutting the belatedly recognised and musically erudite *Machine Gun Etiquette* in 1978. (RA)

SAM DEES

Idolised by hardcore devotees, yet largely unacknowledged outside of southern soul circles, Sam Dees is probably his genre's greatest cult hero. The handful of records that he has made in 40 years of recording show only a small part of a talent that has written and sung some of the finest black American music of the twentieth century. His prodigious writing ability is reflected by the fact that his songs have been recorded by Gladys Knight, Thelma Jones, Rockie Robbins, Larry Graham, Whitney Houston and countless others, to general acclaim.

Dees' song demos have been revered to the same degree as his commercial recordings, and Ace boasts two CDs of these small, but perfectly formed, masterpieces on its Kent subsidary. Dees continues to write great material, and his services are as in demand now as they have been in the past five decades. (TR)

DION DIMUCCI

Dion DiMucci first came to prominence in the late 1950s with his vocal group the Belmonts and a selection of seminal hits such as "Runaround Sue" and "The Wanderer" on Laurie Records. A major label deal with Columbia was intended as a step-up to a Sinatra-style career, but instead led Dion to New York's underbelly of blues and folk clubs. Although this was a personal dead end, it resulted in some revolutionary music. A spiritual rebirth in the late 1960s saw new hits, and a series of records throughout the 1970s became increasingly influential; including the seminal collaboration with Phil Spector, *Born To Be With You*. (DR)

DORIS DUKE

Prior to 1969, female soul singers tended to either focus on the joy of being in love, or the pain of not. They barely focused on pride in infidelity, happiness in divorce or descent from battered wifedom to prostitution. This changed with the release of *I'm a Loser*—masterminded by R&B maverick Jerry 'Swamp Dogg' Williams Jr and rendered real by New Jersey-born Doris Willingham (aka Doris Duke).

Duke's knowing tone brought real life to Williams' adult repertoire, such as "To the Other Woman (I'm the Other Woman)" and "I Don't Care Anymore". The album was as devastating as it was influential, immediately becoming the all time favourite of many deep soul aficionados.

Unfortunately, Duke's record label went bust while the album was in the charts, and she never regained the momentum that her career lost as a result. However, *I'm a Loser* provided the starting point for the likes of Millie Jackson's explicit and brave work of the 1970s, and Duke herself remains a heroine to all soul lovers—as the demand for her expanded *I'm a Loser* Kent CD continues to demonstrate. (TR)

DYKE & THE BLAZERS

Arlester 'Dyke' Christian and his band, the Blazers, are second only to James Brown as trail-blazing avatars of funk. The funk fraternity—from hipster DJs the world over that spin Dyke classics like "We Got More Soul", "Let A Woman Be a Woman" and his 1966 hit "Funky Broadway", to the hip-hop and rap producers who raid the Blazers' grooves for beats—all know full well that Dyke was an artist with a pervasive and undeniable hand in the transformation of R&B into funk. Dyke took the real beat of the street and brought it to the masses—and the street was where he was to die prematurely, at the hands of a drug dealer in 1971. (AP)

EDDIE AND ERNIE

Male duos have always been at the heart of 1960s soul, from Sam & Dave to Sam and Bill, to Pic and Bill and any permutations thereof. However, the collector's choice

among the numerous 'double dynamites' is Edgar 'Eddie' Campbell and Ernie Johnson, who emerged from Arizona in the mid-1960s to fashion a fistful of passionately-delivered gospel soul masterpieces for a variety of important R&B imprints. The duo deserved the same variety of fame as Sam & Dave, but they did not stay long enough with any one imprint to build their profile to the size it deserved. The devoted were prepared to follow them anywhere that their travels took them, and their latter day championing by the late Dave Godin via Kent's *Deep Soul Treasures* series—and a superb Kent CD of their own—finally brought the acclaim they deserved. (TR)

JOHN FAHEY

Scholar, researcher, enthusiast, record label owner, but most of all, phenomenally influential musician, John Fahey elevated the steel-string guitar to the level of a concert instrument. From his first recorded outings on Fonotone 78s as Blind Thomas in 1958, he built a spectacular body of work over some 40 years—mostly for his own Takoma Records and later for Vanguard. Ever the eccentric, he made his first LP, *Blind Joe Death*, in a limited run of 100, going on to re-record most of it twice. He died in 2001, rightly adamant that he was never a folk or new age musician. (RA)

FATBACK BAND

Like a potted history of their time, the Fatback Band went from the loose street funk of their debut album *Keep On Steppin'* to thunderous disco in a nine year career (a period in which they produced 16 albums for the label). Along the way they created rap. They did all this without a permanent lead singer or, indeed, a permanent band.

Bill Curtis and Gerry Thomas wrote and produced most of the music, bringing in the appropriate musicians as the sound dictated. This was their genius and what kept them sounding fresh and up-to-the-minute with the shifting musical fashions of the day. Even today, the Fatback sound is still guaranteed to shake booties on dance floors the world over. (RA)

THE FIREBALLS

The Fireballs had many hits over a long period, first as an instrumental band, then as vocalists. They moved with the times—straddling many styles while still staying largely true to the same Tex-Mex roots as Buddy Holly (with whom they shared the same manager-producer in Norman Petty).

Starting out as a rockabilly band in West Texas in the late 1950s, they switched to instrumentals when their original vocalist quit, and notched up hits such as "Torquay", "Quite a Party" and "Bulldog" prior to teaming up with vocalist Jimmy Gilmer and scoring an American number one with "Sugar Shack" in 1963. From there, they became an American beat band and were called upon to overdub backings onto posthumous Buddy Holly hits such as "Wishing" and "Brown Eyed Handsome Man".

In 1968, they came back strong with another Top 10 hit, "Bottle of Wine", and developed a more progressive outlook, while remaining essentially a vehicle for lead guitarist and founder member George Tomsco. One of the longest associations with Ace, every last note recorded by the Fireballs during the first decade of their existence is available through the label. (RF)

THE FUGS

One of the earliest collisions between an art-boho sensibility and garage folk-rock, the beatnik itinerants who founded The Fugs had no desire for a career but, nevertheless, fashioned a notorious and ultimately influential brand of tantalisingly offensive rock'n'roll. These crazy New Yorkers—poets and existentialists with nary a musician among them—had caused a sensation on the West Coast even before the release of their first album in 1965, which featured such classics as "Boobs a Lot" and "I Couldn't Get High". The Fugs would certainly improve musically over an ensuing, long-lived career, but never once lost their charmingly anarchic edge. (AP)

LOWELL FULSON

Born on a Choctaw Indian reservation near Tulsa Oklahoma on 31 March 1921, Fulson—with his deep baritone voice and rich dark melismatic timbre—was one of the most distinctive blues vocalists on record. A self taught guitarist, he had gained valuable experience playing with the territory bands of Dan Wright and Texas Alexander by his late teens.

After being discharged from military service, circa 1940s, he started a band with his brother Martin. In 1946, they began recording for Bob Geddins and released records on Big Town and Trilon. Geddins sold some of these masters to Jack Lauderdale who released them on his Los Angeles Downbeat label. In 1948, Fulson recorded his first big hit "Three O'clock Blues" for Down Town records (also run by Geddins), which was later covered by BB King. Shortly after, he signed to the Swingtime label where he soon had a huge hit with "Everyday I Have the Blues". By this time, he was an established act, playing with musicians like Lloyd Glenn, Maxell Davis, Jay McShann and Ray Charles, in shows that consistently sold out.

Lowell continued releasing records and performing live until the Swingtime label folded in late 1953. He signed with Aladdin but, within a year, had moved on to Checker where, in 1954, he scored one of his most influential and biggest hits; "Reconsider Baby".

One of Fulson's most productive periods commenced when he signed with Modern Records (of Los Angeles) in 1964 and had almost immediate success with a string of hit singles including "Tramp", "Black Nights", "Too Many Drivers", "Talkin' Woman" and "Shattered Dreams". He continued to record and tour through the 1970s, 80s and 90s. He died on 6 March 1999 at his Long Beach home at the age of 77. (TC)

FUNKADELIC

George Clinton, and his various merry bands, cut eight albums for Westbound Records through the 1970s. Adventurous, absurd, at times hysterical, and always outrageous, their outlandish image is in danger of masking the sheer brilliance of their material and their ability to play. Funkadelic's unmistakable sound is undoubtedly 'black music', but not as anyone had ever heard it before, either lyrically or musically: cosmic guitar solos, spectacular vocal pyrotechnics, sound collages and always those sly observations of the world around us. (RA)

DANA GILLESPIE

Dana Gillespie is Britain's most successful female blues singer and currently has five CDs on release on Ace (for whom she has been recording for over 20 years). Gillespie was born on in London, 30 March 1949, and developed an interest in the blues when she was just 13, on seeing the first American Folk Blues Festival Tour concert in Croydon. While still in her early teens, she went to performances by such British blues bands as The Yardbirds, play at the Crawdaddy in Richmond and other London clubs.

At the age of 15, she started singing in folk clubs and cut her first record "Donna Donna" for Pye in 1965, with Donovan providing the guitar backing. Later that year she was back in the studio—this time with Jimmy Page

on guitar—to record a more 'poppy' second single for the label; "Thank You Boy". Throughout the 1960s, Gillespie continued to record more singles as well as two albums for Decca. She then spent several years concentrating on her acting career (which included starring roles in several West End musicals) until, in 1972, she provided the backing vocals for David Bowie on the *Ziggy Stardust* album.

Bowie repaid the favour by producing a few tracks for Gillespie's first RCA album, *Weren't Born A Man* in 1973, and she subsequently signed with Mainman, the company that managed Bowie at this time. After a second RCA album *Ain't Gonna Play No Second Fiddle*, she moved to New York and toured extensively, as well as hosting a local blues radio show in New York. She returned to London in the early 1980s and started performing with her own blues band. In 1982 she cut her first album for Ace; the wonderful, and slightly *risqué*, "Blue Job".

Since then, Gillespie has continued to work prolifically, touring Europe (in various blues and boogie shows), as well as India (with her blues band) in 2002. She has also developed an interest in Indian and Arabic music, which led to a smash hit single in Europe "Move Your Body Close To Me". In recent years, she has also recorded several albums in Sanskrit, as well as continuing to perform the blues in music festivals throughout the world. (TC)

THE GOSDIN BROTHERS

To the fans of his 1970s and 80s hard country hits, Vern Gosdin is known as 'the voice'. Little known is that those same pipes had earlier graced a remarkable, and prescient, set of country rock recordings in the late 1960s. This was a period when Vern and his brother Rex harmonised effortlessly together, accompanied by a crack session crew (including future Byrd Clarence White), which was assembled by producer Gary Paxton for his Bakersfield International label. The duo's incandescent 1968 album *Sounds of Goodbye* is filled with exemplary songs and performances, and remains a firm favourite at Ace Towers. (AP)

BUDDY GUY

Buddy Guy is probably the most influential electric blues guitar player in music. His influence on countless guitarists, famous or otherwise, is immense. Eric Clapton, Jeff Beck and Jimmy Page all hold him in great esteem. Jimi Hendrix learnt much of his style and showmanship from him and Stevie Ray Vaughan was never slow to acknowledge his debt to the guitarist.

Guy's biggest influence was the legendary Eddie 'Guitar Slim' Jones, who he saw play at the age of 13 in a club in Baton Rouge, Louisiana. Jones clearly made an enormous impression on the young Guy, as he later adopted many of the hallmarks of his flamboyant live act—the long guitar lead, allowing him to commence his act off-stage, the loud clothes and the distorted volume on his guitar.

Buddy Guy was born on 30 July 1936 near the small town of Lettsworth, just a few miles from the infamous Angola Prison Farm and 40 miles North West of Baton Rouge. He started playing guitar on a homemade two-stringed piece of wood and obtained his first real guitar at the age of 17. In September 1957, Buddy moved north to Chicago and, within weeks, had started playing at the 708 club. His first record release was with Cobra Records, but he soon came under the wing of Muddy Waters, who introduced him to Chess Records (where he spent many frustrating years not securing a release under his own name, despite being one of the most in-demand session players on the label). Leonard Chess felt uncomfortable with the level of volume Guy utilised on his records and it was years later in the late 1960s—as he watched Hendrix and Beck achieve huge success with licks, feedback and distortion inspired by Guy—that Chess acknowledged his mistake.

By this time, Guy had secured a deal with Vanguard Records where he cut several successful albums and established a career. However, the 1970s would not prove to be a successful decade for him, despite working and recording prolifically (mostly in partnership with the harmonica wizard, Junior Wells, who had been recording with for Delmark since the mid-1960s). In the late 1980s, Guy was invited to support Clapton for a selection of his shows at the Royal Albert Hall in London. It was at this time that Andrew Lauder signed him to Silvertone Records—the label that he still records for today. In recent years, Guy has finally achieved the, long overdue, recognition he deserves—winning five Grammies, 23 WC Handy awards and, in 2005, induction into the Rock'n'Roll Hall of Fame. (TC)

ISAAC HAYES

A phenomenon by any standards, Isaac Hayes tore up the rulebook when he sold enormous quantities of *Hot Buttered Soul*. Four extended tracks, two of which reworked familiar pop material beyond recognition, was a risky approach in 1969—the genius was no one saw it coming.

Hayes had been at Stax for many years preceding 1969, writing and producing with David Porter (and becoming the men behind Sam & Dave's huge success, among other things). His debut album *Presenting Isaac Hayes* had been released the year before without causing much of a stir, so no one could have been prepared for the career to follow.

In 1971 he scored the first of three movies while at Stax. *Shaft*, the soundtrack, was far more successful than the movie—the title track still thrills. The legacy of Hayes' Stax albums is that they still sound fresh—an achievement that few have been able to imitate. (RA)

JOHN LEE HOOKER

John Lee Hooker was a complete original, whose primal blues hark back to an era before he first started recording himself (in 1948). The earliest recordings he made are on Ace, as are later sides cut for Modern, Specialty, Riverside and, later in the catalogue, for Stax. Before his death, in June 2001, he was still making records with that unrivalled ability to evoke a mood and tell a story. For more information about his immense recording career, see Charles Shaar Murray's definitive biography *Boogie Man: Adventures of John Lee Hooker in the American 20th Century* (London: Penguin, 2000). (RA)

IKE AND TINA TURNER

Ike Turner was born in Clarksdale Mississippi on 5 November 1931. His interest in music was kindled at the age of eight, when he began assisting a DJ on the local radio station WROX. Turner was inspired by guitarist, Robert Nighthawk, and pianist, Pinetop Perkins, both of whom he encountered while at WROX. Before long, he had become proficient on both guitar and piano and, while still at high school, started his own band; the legendary Kings of Rhythm.

In 1950, BB King arranged for Turner and his band to record at Sam Philips' Sun recording studio in Memphis. On the journey from Clarksdale to Memphis they wrote "Rocket 88", now regarded as one of the first ever rock'n'roll records. The release became an instant smash, but was issued under the name of the band's vocalist, saxophonist Jackie Brenston.

During the next few years, Turner continued playing with the band as well as working, for a short spell, as a talent scout for Modern Records (as sidekick to Joe Bihari)—recording local talent throughout Mississippi and Arkansas in 1951 and in 1952. He also worked as a musician on many of these records and can be heard playing piano on some of Howling Wolf's earliest recordings. In 1954, Turner moved to St Louis where he worked the clubs and recorded for local labels until, in 1958, he met the 18 year old Anna Mae Bullock and hired her as a backing singer. Soon, 'Little Ann' was a featured performer with the band and she and Turner commenced a relationship.

When a male vocalist failed to show for a recording session for Sue Records in late 1959, Little Ann stepped in and recorded the song "Fool in Love". The rest is history. On release in 1960, the record shot to number two in the R&B chart and number 27 in the pop chart, following an appearance on American Bandstand. With "Fool in Love" Little Ann was transformed into 'Tina Turner'. The following year, 'Ike and Tina Turner' charted with "I Think It's Gonna Work Out Fine", and swiftly became a major attraction—rivalled only by James Brown as the top act on the chittlin circuit. In 1964, Ike and Tina Turner signed with Modern records and had a big hit with "I Can't Believe What You Say", in addition to recording several albums. In 1966, Tina recorded the classic "River Deep, Mountain High" produced by Phil Spector for his own Philles label. The pair continued to have major hits in the 1970s with "Proud Mary" and the classic "Nutbush City Limits" (written by Tina). However, the constant touring and recording took its toll: the relationship broke down in 1975 when Tina walked out on Ike for good. (TC)

THE IMPRESSIONS

Not only did Curtis Mayfield, Sam Gooden and Fred Cash write the book about group soul, they edited it and autographed its first edition. Their combination of warm harmonies, and the unique voice and songs of Mayfield, made The Impressions a living template for hundreds of lesser acts across the USA—and as many again in Jamaica, where their records and abiding influence helped to shape the genre that came to be know as rocksteady.

From the start of his song writing career, Mayfield's lyrics often concerned themselves with weightier topics than love and romance, prefacing and providing the catalyst for more socially conscious works of the late 1960s such as Marvin Gaye's "What's Going On". Mayfield also wrote great songs for a host of important contemporaries—Gene Chandler, Major Lance, Walter Jackson, and so on—but he almost always saved the best for himself, Gooden and Cash.

The Impressions' complete ABC Paramount recordings from 1961 to 1968—generally considered to be their finest overall body of work—are all available, across a selection of 'must have' Kent CDs. (TR)

CHUCK JACKSON

With a lengthy string of urbane R&B hits that included "I Don't Want To Cry", "I Wake Up Crying", "Any Day Now (My Wild Beautiful Bird)" and "Tell Him I'm Not Home", all cut in New York for Florence Greenberg's Wand label in 1962, Chuck Jackson established himself as one the first and greatest stars of soul.

Born in Latta, South Carolina on 22 July 1937, like many of his contemporaries he began his career as a gospel performer and also recorded in the late 1950s as a member of the Dell-Vikings, before going solo. He also notched up a few charters in duet with Maxine Brown before jumping ship to Motown in 1969, where he registered with "Are You Lonely For Me Baby" and "Honey Come Back". Jackson's last hit, "I Wanna Give You Some Love" in the 1980s, was written by Bob Marley. (MP)

MILLIE JACKSON

The phrase "telling it like it is" could have been coined purely for Millie Jackson. Her notorious raps certainly pull no punches as she lays into both sides of the sex war with equal abandon. But more than that, Jackson is one of the great female soul singers. Originally from Georgia, she initially found fame with the New York-based Spring Records, cutting 16 studio albums, including the steaming *Royal Rappin's* with Isaac Hayes. There were also two sensational live albums (available as one double CD), that catch Millie at her sassy best, indeed telling it like it is for an enraptured audience: an extraordinary woman and an exceptional talent. (RA)

WANDA JACKSON

By the age of 20, Wanda Jackson had toured the South with the young Elvis, worked country shows with Johnny Cash, Gene Vincent and Jerry Lee Lewis, and made some of the hottest and sexiest rock'n'roll sides by any female artist from that era—records that captured the zeitgeist of the times more convincingly than many a better known hit.

By the mid-60s, she had come into her own as a country star but she never moved to Nashville, although it might have helped her career, and she didn't sell out. Nor did she lose her rebel spirit, the identifying trait that continues to endear her to a following among younger people (which many other survivors from that era can only envy). She is the last of the 'red hot mamas' and an American legend. (RF)

JAMES TAYLOR QUARTET

The James Taylor Quartet formed from the ashes of The Prisoners, and went on to become one of Britain's most successful jazz and soul outfits of the past two decades. Their first release, a punk jazz version of Herbie Hancock's "Blow Up", was a massive indie hit that led to their signing to Polydor's Urban label. It was here that they found success with their classic version of "Starsky and Hutch". By the early 1990s, they were achieving chart hits and were one of the most exciting live acts of the time. Re-signing to the Acid Jazz label in 1994, they released their biggest selling album to date, the soul and jazz cornucopia *In the Hand of the Inevitable*. (DR)

ELMORE JAMES

The slide guitar riff that launched a thousand blues revivalists may not have originated with Canton, MS finest, but few have ever been quite so indelibly identified with a signature lick than Elmore James, with "Dust My Broom". It provided a motif that cropped up time and time again throughout his all-too-short career, which ceased prematurely in 1963 when he died of heart problems. It provided an inspiration for the early work of a generation of British and American blues guitarists, from Eric Clapton and Peter Green to Mike Bloomfield and Johnny Winter. Of course, there was much more to Elmore than one almighty riff, and the full breadth of his repertoire—from rhumba boogies to proto-doo-wop—is displayed across the recordings he made for Flair and Meteor in the early to mid-1950s, all enshrined in the CD boxed set on Ace. (TR)

CECILE KAYIREBWA

Cecile Kayirebwa was always immersed in the diverse music of her country Rwanda, regardless of tribal or social standing. Aged 15 she became a founding member of the Rwanda Song and Dance Circle. Later, as a welfare officer, she was afforded the opportunity to travel and absorb the poetry and song of the entire country. She relocated to Belgium in 1973, studied music there at the Royal Museum of Central Africa and formed the group Inyange. Over the next ten years she released a series of cassettes and these were compiled into a *GlobeStyle* CD in 1994. She has continued to tour and record. (RA)

ALBERT KING

From Indianola, deep in the Mississippi Delta, (the same town as his namesake, BB King), Albert King was 30 before he cut his first session for Parrot Records in 1953, but had already paid his dues for several years at the T-99 Club in Osceola, Arkansas. Moving to St Louis, he had a spell with Bobbin Records, later absorbed by Sid Nathan's King. However, it was at Stax that he finally found fame, fortune and hit records—from 1966 to its bitter demise ten years later. King remained one of the three great kings of the blues guitar until his untimely demise in 1992. (RA)

BB KING

BB King is, without a doubt, the undisputed 'chairman' of the 'Board of Blues Incorporated'. In his eightieth year, he is now more popular than ever. Embraced by the young bucks of the rock scene as a patriarch, his easy manner, sweet and high vocals and stinging guitar add up to a sophisticated style that has endured longer than most careers already. Ace represent the sides he cut for the Modern's RPM and Crown labels. See the box set, *The Vintage Years*, for a superb overview of his early years. (RA)

FREDDY KING

Freddy King was one of the most influential Blues guitarists of all time. Some of his early recordings, notably "Hideaway", were released in Britain and drew him to the attention of many young British blues musicians, including Peter Green, Eric Clapton, John Mayall, Jeff Beck, Stan Webb and Jimmy Page. Realising the appeal of King's music for white kids, King Records repackaged some of his instrumental sides in the early 1960s in an album entitled *Freddy King Goes Surfin'*.

King was born in Gilmer, Texas on 3 September 1934. There were several guitarists in his family and he began playing the instrument at the age of six. He moved to Chicago with his family in 1950 and was soon listening to artists like T-Bone Walker, Elmore James, Muddy Waters and Howlin' Wolf.

In 1953, he cut his first sides for the Parrot label, but it was not until 1960 that he signed to the Federal label, a subsidiary of King Records in Cincinnati on the recommendation of pianist Sonny Thompson (with who he was to work and write during his tenure at King). One of his first recordings for Federal was the instrumental "Hideaway" which, on release, became an instant top ten smash in the R&B chart and reached number 29 in the pop chart.

From this time on, King was a success, and became a major attraction on the chittlin circuit as well as playing to, largely white, college audiences. In 1963, he left Chicago and moved back to Texas to live with his wife and children. In 1966 he left Federal Records and released two albums with Cotillion before moving on to Shelter. Later, Clapton arranged for him to sign with the RSO label. King toured extensively in the late 1960s and 70s until his tragic death from a heart attack in Dallas in 1976—he was just 42 years of age. (TC)

LINK WRAY

Link Wray was born on 2 May 1929 in Dunn, North Carolina, and learned guitar at the age of eight from a carnival musician named Hambone. He moved to Norfolk, Virginia, in the mid-1940s where he began playing in various hillbilly bands. After having a serious operation as a result of contracting TB, Wray returned to the road in the 1950s, joining forces with his brothers in a band for which he played lead guitar. In 1958, he recorded the influential instrumental hit "Rumble" for the Cadence label. In the 1960s he cut more hits for Epic and

Swan until, tired of touring, he set up a three track studio on the family farm in Maryland—where he would record a slew of atmospheric country rock tracks that eventually found release in the early 1970s. After working with Robert Gordon in the late 1970s, Wray came into contact with Ace Records for the first time. From 1982 to 1995, he recorded six albums in total for the label. One of the most seminally influential rock'n'roll guitarists, Wray lived a relatively quiet life in Denmark with his wife and son until he died in November 2005. (TC)

MARY LOVE

Love was the first voice to be heard on the Kent label when her northern soul classic "You Turned My Bitter Into Sweet" opened the first side of the *For Dancers Only* LP in 1982. She had a string of classic 1960s soul recordings for LA's Modern label and her "Lay This Burden Down", apart from being a perennial northern dancefloor filler, has been re-mixed by several inspired soulful house DJs. She continued to record into the 1980s and beyond, but mainly gospel tracks since the late 1970s. One of these—"Come Out of the Sandbox"—was adopted by the modern soul crowd at Southport Weekenders and is a soul anthem to their educated ears. (AC)

LONNIE MACK

Lonnie Mack burst out of Cincinnati in 1963 with his blistering instrumental take on Chuck Berry's "Memphis, Tennessee", and immediately won the hearts of disfranchised rockers and blues enthusiasts alike. His reputation as an innovative axe man was quickly enhanced by a selection of vocal sides demonstrating that he had listened to all the right R&B and gospel records as a youth. Throughout the 1960s, his 45s were mostly mandatory purchases, whether vocal or instrumental. Mack's unbeatable guitar playing was invariably enhanced by the unique 'wobbly' sound that came through his amplifier and, if he was not the very first guitarist to use a Magnatone, then he was certainly among the first to use it so identifiably. He still makes great records—all of which are available on Ace. (TR)

JIMMY MCCRACKLIN

Veteran bluesman, Jimmy McCracklin, was born on 13 August 1921 in St Louis. He made his first record "Miss Mattie Left Me" for the Globe label in 1945. He recorded for Swingtime and Modern Records during the 1940s, moving briefly to Peacock in the early 1950s, before returning to Modern with the Blues Blasters (featuring Lafayette Thomas on guitar) where he cut many of his great sides.

In 1958, while playing a club date in Chicago, McCracklin recorded a solo, "The Walk", and dropped the tape off at Chess Records. On release, it became a massive hit on both the R&B and pop charts—bringing his name to a worldwide audience following its international release. Although a prolific songwriter (he wrote "Tramp" for his buddy Lowell Fulson), McCracklin was unable to make a successful follow-up to "The Walk".

He started the Art-Tone label in 1961 and, shortly after, scored a number two hit in the R&B charts with another of his own compositions, "I Gotta Know". Since then, McCracklin has recorded for many different labels, including Stax. Today, he still tours regularly with a nine piece band and has been to Europe several times in recent years. (TC)

MOTORHEAD

Motorhead fans worldwide revere Chiswick Records for releasing the band's first album when no one else was interested. *Motorhead*, the first album, heralded a career that is still going strong 30 years later, as well as the launch of a new musical genre, speed metal. Lemmy Kilmister (born Stoke-On-Trent, 24 December 1945), the founder and last serving original member of this Grammy award-winning metal combo, left his previous band Hawkwind after a misunderstanding with overzealous Canadian customs officers.

He was determined to create the "loudest, nastiest, most in your face" band ever and, it has to be said, he did a pretty good job. The classic Chiswick line-up of Motorhead—Kilmister, Fast Eddie Clark and Phil Taylor—evolved after a series of disappointments, reneged promises and aborted record releases that had resulted in the band being branded 'losers' and 'troublesome' by the music industry. Enter Chiswick Records. Just as the band was about to disintegrate, Chiswick enabled Motorhead to record their initial album—launching the band's successful and highly influential career. (TC)

MOON MULLICAN

The Decca and King records that Aubrey Mullican made were often years ahead of their time, and those he cut with Boyd Bennett's Rockets in 1956—especially "Seven Nights to Rock"—were as authentic as anything being pounded out in Memphis by the young whippersnapper, Jerry Lee Lewis. He reached a peak at King in the late 1940s with gems like "Don't Ever Take My Picture Down", "Cherokee Boogie" and the original version of Hank Williams' hit "Jambalaya". Ace's catalogue boasts two CDs that cover all of Mullican's best King moments. (TR)

THE MUSIC MACHINE

Thanks to a foreboding monochromatic image, The Music Machine is often termed a garage band, but in truth they simply do not sound like anyone else, that came either before or after them. "Talk Talk", their ode to the social lack of self-esteem, hit the American Top 20 in December 1966 and was housed in a complex, dance-defying beat—rendered with a brutal sonic punch. Front man and songwriter, Sean Bonniwell, provided a wealth of similarly thought-provoking material for the band's subsequent record career which, despite a lack of success, stand today as some of the most powerful and intelligent rock records made. (AP)

JACK NITZSCHE

Jack Nitzsche first came to prominence orchestrating Phil Spector's "little symphonies for the kids", and established a reputation as one of the most in demand arrangers in early 1960s Hollywood. Nitzsche was first and foremost a maverick, unafraid to champion outsiders like the Rolling Stones and known as much for his quirks as his abilities. Right up to his death in 2000, Nitzsche was writing, recording and producing a staggering variety of music, from Academy Award-winning soundtracks to neo-classical suites, from Doris Day to Captain Beefheart and the Monkees. He was truly a one-of-a-kind talent. (AP)

OHIO PLAYERS

The Ohio Players' roots go back to Dayton, Ohio. They were originally called the Ohio Untouchables, and before that, the Bees on the absurdly obscure Finch label. They cut sides for Lupine, and backed Wilson Pickett in the Falcons' "I Found a Love". The main players in the Ohio Untouchables eventually left their front man, Robert Ward, recruited new members and became the Ohio Players. They arrived at Westbound via New York and Nashville, hitting immediately with their debut Westbound 45, "Pain". But it was their fourth single; the almost ludicrous and now much sampled "Funky Worm", that took them to

the top. They cut three albums at Westbound, each with the distinctive and distinctly erotic Joel Brodsky sleeve shot. They then moved to Mercury—a string of hits and a considerable amount of litigation followed over the next four years. One group member, Junie Morrison, stayed at Westbound and cut three solo albums, which are anthologised on *The Westbound Years*. (RA)

JOHNNY OTIS

Born 28 December in 1921 in Vallejo, California, Johnny Otis' long career in music confirms that he is one of the most influential figures in the history of R&B. At the age of 18 he began playing drums with Count Otis Mathews' Band in Oakland and, four years later, moved to Los Angeles to get involved in the thriving Central Avenue music scene. After a spell with Harlan Leonard's band at the club, Alabam, he formed his own band and had a first hit "Harlem Nocturne" on Savoy in 1945.

In 1948, he opened the legendary Barrelhouse nightclub with Bardu Ali. During this time, he recorded hit records with vocalists such as 'Little' Esther Philips and Mel Walker. In 1950 he took to the road in a review entitled the California Rhythm & Blues Caravan, becoming one of the hottest acts in R&B during the early 1950s.

Throughout his career, he has discovered and encouraged countless stars, including Big Mama Thornton, Etta James, Hank Ballard, Esther Philips, The Coasters, Big Jay McNeely and Little Willie John, to name but a few. He has run his own record labels and studio, written books, been a successful radio DJ for almost half a century, had his own TV series as well as finding time to be a successful songwriter ("Every Beat of My Heart", "Roll With Me Henry", "So Fine" and "Willie and the Hand Jive"). He got involved in politics for a short period in the early 1960s and served as Deputy Chief of Staff to Democratic Congressman,

Mervin Dymally, who was also Lieutenant Governor of California. Since then, Otis has continued to be active, in a number of creative realms and for the past 15 years has lived in Sebastopol in Northern California. (TC)

THE PRISONERS

The Medway quartet formed at school and went on to record four of the best garage LPs of the 1980s. They were a tremendous live band, whose general flair was augmented by the songwriting and voice of Graham Day. The band achieved ongoing cult status that sees them revered by people such as Noel Gallagher and Tim Burgess and their take on Joe South's "Hush" was appropriated by Kula Shaker for a Top Ten hit. *The Last Fourfathers* is considered to be their masterpiece, but each of their albums is a fantastic and unique listening experience. (DR)

THE RADIATORS

From the sonic assault of 1977's debut 45, "Television Screen", to the finest and most pertinent Irish rock album of all time, *Ghostown*; The Radiators grew massively as a force of music, in a period that covered just two years. For the first time in Irish cultural life, a rock music 33 rpm could sit happily alongside the country's literary and dramatic output. 30 years elapsed during which they busied themselves in production, design and the retention of artistic integrity. In 2006 they returned with another great record suffused with politics—both personal and universal. (RA)

BUFFY SAINTE-MARIE

Singer and songwriter, Buffy Sainte-Marie, is one of the most well known Native American performers in pop.

Many in Britain were introduced to her work via the Donovan cover version of "Universal Soldier", an affecting and moving commentary on those who must go to war. For many others, her performance of the title track to the harrowing—but brilliant—film *Soldier Blue* was the starting point. She easily mixes originals with covers and displays a broad range of styles across these Vanguard albums. The distinctive mouthbow playing is a signature of her recordings, and she produces a remarkable range of sound from it. (RA)

ROCKY SHARPE

Rocky Sharpe and the Replays evolved from an earlier incarnation, Rocky Sharpe and The Razors, an 11 piece rock'n'roll revival band which included some members of the Darts and who had released an EP on the Chiswick label in 1976. The Replays were Rocky Sharpe (Robert Podsiadly), Johnny Stud (Jan Podsiadly), Helen Highwater (Helen Blizard) and Eric Rondo (Mike Vernon). They scored a huge international hit in 1978 with a brilliant remake of the old Edsels' recording "Rama Lama Ding Dong", which was produced by Pete Wingfield, and showed off Sharpe's remarkable vocal skills to the full. The group followed up with several other international hits including "Imagination", "Martian Hop", "Shout Shout" and "Love Will Make You Fail In School".

Rocky Sharpe and the Replays scored seven hit singles altogether, and recorded three albums, before disbanding in 1984. They toured with their backing band, the Topliners, and appeared on a myriad of television shows throughout Europe, including an edition of the top German programme, *Music Laden*, with the Pointer Sisters, Chic, the Jacksons and many other major stars of the day. Sadly, Sharpe is now beset by multiple sclerosis—otherwise he could still be enjoying a good touring career on the European circuit, particularly in Spain. (TC)

THE SOFT MACHINE

One of Ace Records' biggest selling titles, this seminal British prog-psych outfit's first pair of LPs is testament to the quirky edge the group had in their earliest incarnation(s). The Canterbury legend's first album, recorded while on tour in America in 1968, and not issued in Britain until Big Beat licensed it in the 1980s, features the spiky song-craft of founder member Kevin Ayers; its sequel introduced another bass-playing writing talent, Hugh Hopper. On both sets, the inventive keyboard of Mike Ratledge and distinctive voice of Robert Wyatt seal the enduring appeal of this cornerstone outfit. (AP)

THE SONICS

More renowned now than at any time during their relatively short-lived career of the mid-1960s, the Sonics took rock'n'roll by the scruff of the neck and thrashed it to within an inch of its life, leaving a legacy of some of the most savage, visceral recordings ever made. Emerging from the same Pacific northwest wellspring as the Wailers and Ventures, the group's incendiary singles from 1964 and 1965, such as "The Witch" and "Psycho", proved inspirational to punk in 1977 and grunge in the late 1980s, as well as influencing the recent crop of born-again garage rockers. (AP)

THE STAPLE SINGERS

"Our theme is love, freedom and peace" said Roebuck 'Pops' Staples, and for just shy of 50 years until his death in 2000, the Staple Singers practised what he preached. The story of family act (sisters Cleotha, Yvonne, Mavis and, at times, brother Pervis) took them from a pure gospel outfit in the 1950s, to the creators of soul-folk and involvement in the Civil Rights movement in the 1960s and the monumentally influential series of Stax 45s like "I'll Take You There" and

"Respect Yourself" in the 1970s. Like the liquid shimmer of Pop's guitar, they reverberate to this day. (RA)

SHARON TANDY

Sharon Tandy was a gifted vamp from Johannesburg whose mid-1960s oeuvre straddles spectacular British-girl pop ("Perhaps Not Forever"), wigged-out freakbeat ("Hold On") and authentic, Memphis-recorded blue-eyed soul ("Toe Hold"). While she may have been shy, she was adept at all. Significant as the first foreigner signed directly to the Stax label—Tandy opened shows on the legendary British Stax-Volt tour in 1967. Tandy's career never took off as it should, but today she is revered as a mod goddess—with Big Beat Records anthologising her work on the best-selling *You Gotta Believe It's... Sharon Tandy*. (AP)

IRMA THOMAS

Otherwise known as "The Soul Queen of New Orleans", Irma Thomas' recording of the immortal "Time is on my Side"—while not being the original—is the definitive version, and the template for the Rolling Stones' song of the same title. Thomas was born Irma Lee on 18 February 1941 in Ponchatoula, Louisiana, and raised in the Crescent City. She debuted with "Don't Mess With My Man" on Ron, an R&B hit in 1960. Switching to Minit Records, she worked closely with the legendary songwriter/producer, Allen Toussaint, on classics such as "It's Raining" and "Ruler of my Heart" (the latter subsequently reworked by Otis Redding as "Pain in my Heart"). In 1964, Thomas began a three-year stint with Imperial Records, with the self-penned and autobiographical "Wish Someone Would Care", the biggest hit of her career. She went on to record for Chess, Canyon, Roker, Cotillion, Fungus and other labels, eventually settling at Rounder Records where, in 1990, she delivered *My Heart's In Memphis*, a tremendous album of Dan Penn compositions, vintage and new. In 2005, her home and her nightclub, the Lion's Den, were submerged by Hurricane Katrina. Undaunted, Thomas returned the following year with *After The Rain*, her last album to date. (MP)

RUFUS THOMAS

The self-confessed, oldest teenager in the business; Rufus Thomas' career stretches way back to the days of the minstrel shows where he started out. He cut records for Modern and Sun before arriving at Stax and proceeded to dance his way through more than a decade of hits for the label. He was a terrific blues singer, and a master entertainer. (RA)

THE WAILERS

Grandaddies of the entire Pacific Northwest rock scene—Tacoma's The Wailers debuted in 1958 with the classic instrumental "Tall Cool One" and went on to forge their own resolutely 'rocking' path. Showcasing the incomparable talents of vocalist Kent Morrill and guitarist Rich Dangel, the combo bucked convention by establishing their own record label, Etiquette, and led by example with a cathartic stage show. Though they made many superb records in their decade together, The Wailers' greatest gift to rock'n'roll was the definitive "Louie Louie". (AP)

LARRY WILLIAMS

The real life 'bad boy' of rock'n'roll, Larry Williams lived a private life that was said to be as fast and loose as the killer cuts that he made for Specialty Records. The music was invariably as wild and crazy as the man himself, and carried influence that reached far beyond his meagre chart tally (especially with people such as John Lennon, whose

popular beat combo covered no less than three of Larry's prime cuts on The Beatles earlier albums). Williams was one of the few who was able to make a wholly successful transition to soul music in the mid-1960s via a string of great 45s that were often cut with his contemporary Johnny 'Guitar' Watson. He died, in somewhat less than salubrious circumstances, some years ago but, as long as rock'n'roll and R&B live, so will Williams' stellar recordings. (TR)

RICK(Y) WILSON

Who would have thought that the cute kid from one of America's most loved TV sitcoms of the 1950s could become one of the best and most consistent artists of the rock'n'roll years? 'Little Ricky' might have had the looks of Fabian, but he also had the hillbilly soul of Carl Perkins. Wilson loved rockabilly, and surrounded himself with writers (including Johnny and Dorsey Burnette) and musicians (the former members of Bob Luman's band, including the great James Burton) who could create it authentically. His Imperial 45s were the real deal and earned him the respect of the rock'n'roll hardcore and millions of swooning females in equal measure. The best of them are collected on Ace's *Rockin' With Ricky* CD. (TR)

THE ZOMBIES

The Zombies are one of the few British bands of the 1960s to have enjoyed true global popularity, with two American number ones, chart records throughout the world and a lasting affection for their music from fans young and old. As the acclaimed *Zombie Heaven* box set demonstrates, this St Albans quintet embodied a singular pop archetype with great songs, great players and—in lead singer Colin Blunstone—a voice to die for. The group's 1967 swansong *Odessey and Oracle* is rightly regarded as one of the essential albums of that tumultuous decade. (AP)

ction Name ABERCC RECORD CORP **Address** 1650 Bway

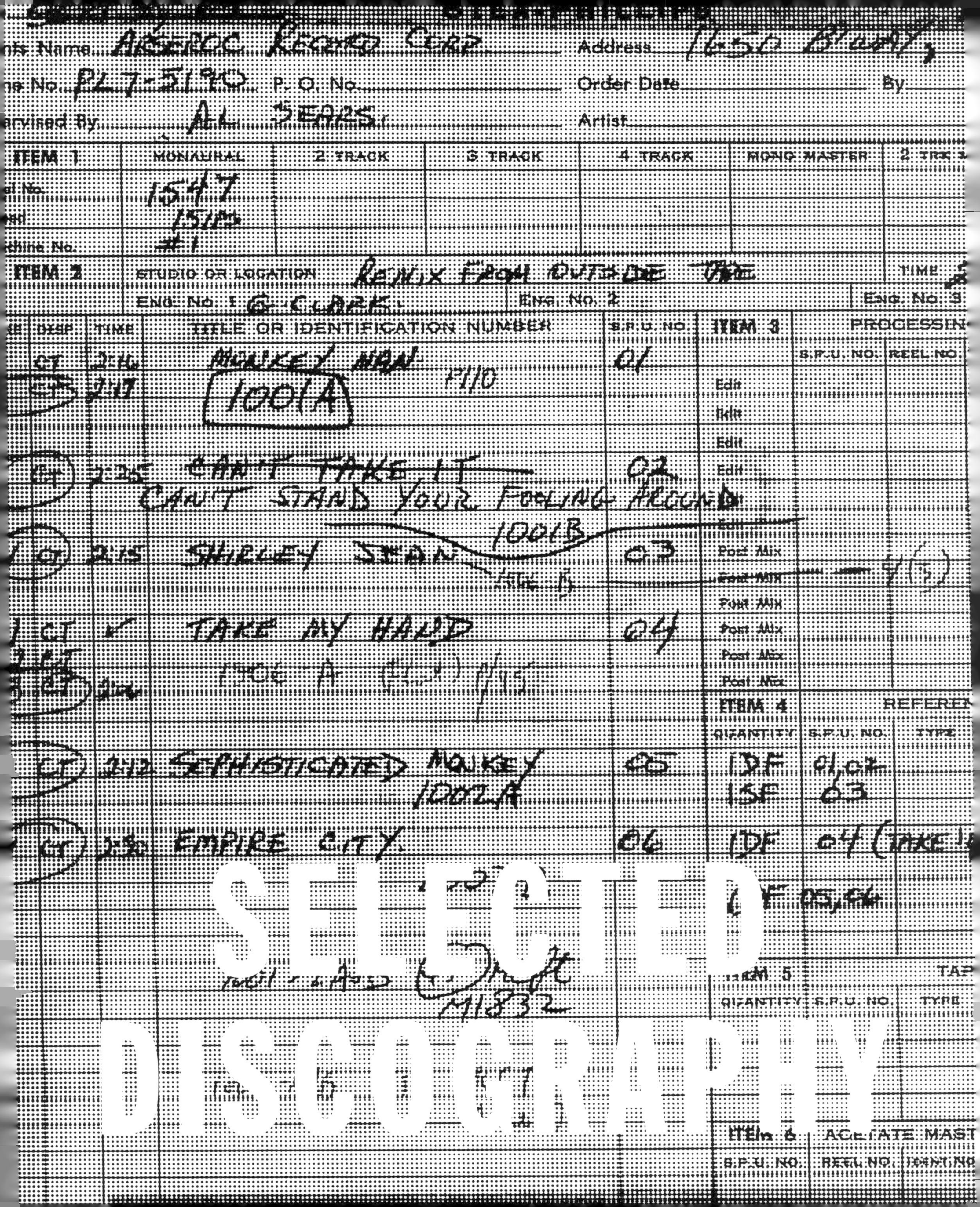

one No. PL7-5190 **P.O. No.** **Order Date** **By**

ervised By AL SEARS **Artist**

ITEM 1	MONAURAL	2 TRACK	3 TRACK	4 TRACK	MONO MASTER	2 TRK
al No.	1547					
sd	1512					
thine No.	#1					

ITEM 2 **STUDIO OR LOCATION** REMIX FROM OUTSIDE TAPE **TIME**

ENG. No. 1 G. CLARK **ENG. No. 2** **ENG. No. 3**

DISP	TIME	TITLE OR IDENTIFICATION NUMBER	S.P.U. NO.	ITEM 3	PROCESSIN
					S.P.U. NO.	REEL NO.
CT	2:40	MONKEY MAN P110	01		
2:17		1001A		Edit	
				Edit	
				Edit	
2:25		CAN'T TAKE IT	02	Edit	
		CAN'T STAND YOUR FOOLING AROUND		Edit	
2:15		SHIRLEY JEAN 1001B	03	Post Mix	7(5)
		SIDE B		Post Mix	
				Post Mix	
CT		TAKE MY HAND	04	Post Mix	
		SIDE A (FLIP) #15		Post Mix	
				Post Mix	

ITEM 4 **REFEREN**

				QUANTITY	S.P.U. NO.	TYPE
CT	2:12	SOPHISTICATED MONKEY 1002A	05	1DF	01,02
				1SF	03
CT	2:30	EMPIRE CITY	06	1DF	04 (TAKE
				DF	05,06

M1332

ITEM 5 **TAP**

QUANTITY **S.P.U. NO.** **TYPE**

ITEM 6 **ACETATE MAST**

S.P.U. NO. **REEL NO.**

SELECTED DISCOGRAPHY

In 1979, the Ace label was created to specialise in old deleted masters sourced from other record companies. It was named after the original Ace Records from Jackson, Mississippi with the permission of Johnny Vincent, the owner of the Jackson-based label from whom Ace had licensed several hundred masters.

At the time, Ace was a subsidiary label of Chiswick Records (Chiswick is now a subsidiary of Ace Records). Ace believes it is good policy to create specific labels that specialise in releasing different music genres. For instance, in 1982, a couple of years after releasing blues, rock'n'roll and rockabilly, Kent Records was initiated, specialising in 1960s music and northern soul. Soon after came Boplicity, which began releasing jazz masters.

Chiswick was issuing pop but, as this label was licensed to EMI, Ace required another label for those records that didn't fit into this mould. So came Big Beat, with whom Johnny and the Jammers released their first 45 and Joe 'King' Carrasco his first LP. It was also the vehicle for reissues of music by 1960s bands such as Soft Machine.

In 1985, came Globestyle Records, which released what became known as 'world music'. In 1987 Beat Goes Public arrived, reissuing the jazz recordings that was enjoying a resurgence in popularity (due to the efforts of young jazz DJs such as Gilles Peterson). In 1989, Ace acquired the masters of Spring Records, but for contractual reasons were unable to use the name 'Spring' itself. They licensed Westbound and Eastbound, and chose Southbound to issue Millie Jackson and the Fatback Band (which were 1970s recordings and thus didn't fit easily onto the Kent label).

There are a myriad of other labels, some licensed-in originals, such as Takoma, Vanguard and Westbound, that Ace continue to licence; and others that were named by Ace itself—Del-Rio and Impact for example—that are all part of the label's story.

Also, as you will see on the following pages, Ace have acquired or licensed a number of independent labels (mostly American) and these are released on whichever Ace label is appropriate to the style or genre of music. For a detailed discography covering every record ever released on Ace or any of its associated labels, see: www.acerecords.co.uk/discography

ACE RECORDS

AROCK

AROCK RECORDS

Div: ARSEROC RECORD CORP.
1650 B'dway. NYC

Rual Music
ASCAP

AR-1003-A
2:19

Arr. by
Lee Porter

Milport
Production

I'M LEAVIN'
(FOR PARTS UNKNOWN)
(Ron Miller & Lee Porter)

GARY & GARY

Fox Family SYLVIA

Sylvia Music
BMI
Time: 2:28

TCF-124
ZTSP 106536

PROMOTIONAL COPY

NOT FOR SALE

A DIVISION OF 20th CENTURY-FOX RECORD CORP. 444 W. 56th ST., N.Y. 10019 MADE IN U.S.A.

I WANNA COME IN
(R. Washington - C. Harper - L. Lucie)

BILLY WASHINGTON

Serock RECORDS

Rual Music Co.
Inc. - ASCAP
Time 2:57

SR 2001
SR-2001-A

A DAY OR TWO
(Ron Miller & Lee Porter)

GARRETT SAUNDERS

A MILLER & PORTER
PRODUCTION

ART

Perfect RECORDS

45-109-A
Time 2:13
45 RPM

ARTREC
(BMI)

HANG LOOSE
(You Gotta Rock)
-Spurlin-Frost-

TOMMY SPURLIN
and the Southern Boys

PRODUCED BY ART RECORDS, INC. MIAMI, FLA., U.S.A. T.M.REG.

COMBO

Combo RECORDS
HOLLYWOOD, CALIF.

127-AA
Combo Music
B.M.I.

Time 2:30

BEANS 'N' GREENS
(J. Porter-J. Green)

THE NUTONES

COMBO

12-B
Time 2:13

Vocal by
John Watson

MOTOR HEAD BABY
(J. Watson V. Haven)

CHUCK HIGGINS
(and His Mellotones)

JOHN WATSON
ELI TONEY
JOE URBERT

DAVE HAMILTON

NEW DAY

DA 102 A
Demoristic Pub.
BMI
Time 2:50
Engineer:
Chico Jones

Arranged &
Produced by:
J. Allen &
D. Hamilton

I GOT SOME
(Hamilton, Allen, Jones, Tolbert)

BILLY (Sugar Billy) GARNER

TEMPLE

2084-A
45 RPM

Demoristic
Pub. Co.-BMI
Time: 2:10

LOVE FRIENDS AND MONEY
(Lately, Hamilton)

JAMES LATELY
2084-A

TCB

Produced by:
D. Hamilton &
O.C. Tolbert

TCB 51
Demoristic Pub.
BMI - 2:24

PISCES PACE
(Dave Hamilton)

DAVE HAMILTON

TCB Recording Studios, 1587 Highland, Detroit, Michigan

DOLPHIN

DOOTONE

AUTHENTIC RECORDS

703-B—45

DOOTSIE WILLIAMS BMI

I WANNA KNOW
(Willie Headen)
WILLIE HEADEN
AND
THE FIVE BIRDS

DOOTONE RECORDS

9514 S. CENTRAL AVE.
LOS ANGELES 2, CALIF.

302-AA
Dootsie Williams
Pub. — B.M.I.

JUMP BLUES NOVELTY
Vocal by
BOBBY NUNN

ANTICIPATING BLUES
(D. Williams-P. Stansel)
BOBBY NUNN
AND
COMBO

Copyright 1951

TONE RECORDS

317-A

DOOTSIE WILLIAMS
PUBLICATIONS—BMI

AUTOMATIC DADDY
(Jones)
VOCAL BY
RESSIE MAE JONES
AND HER
COMBO

DORE-ERA

ERA RECORDS

Reg. U.S. Pat. Off.

45 RPM   45 RPM

(45-HN-112)
NOT FOR SALE

© 1957
Aries Music
BMI 2:13

TOPSY TURVY
(Fred Smith-Clifford Goldsmith)
BENN JOE ZEPPA
AND INSTRUMENTAL GROUP
45-1042

Doré

45 RPM   45 RPM

(45-HN-192)

© 1958
Hillary Music
BMI 2:15

MAXIES MELODY
(ROCK 'N ROLL VERSION)
(Bob Florence)
THE CRUISERS
45-512

Catch RECORDS

REG. U.S. PAT. OFF.

Dist. by
ERA RECORD SALES

Arr.: Jack Nitzsche

(Steven Howard)
Pattern Music,
Inc. (ASCAP)
(BSN-342)

Time 2:19

MUSIC CITY
By
THE PLEASURES
100

DOWNEY

DOWNEY PRODUCTIONS

EXPANDED SOUND

Downey Music
Pub. (BMI)
(D-138-B)

D-138
Time 2:20

PROMOTIONAL
COPY

NOT FOR SALE

WHAT I WANT YOU TO SAY
(Gary Bodily)
THE BARACUDAS
Produced by Bill Wenzel

Leo

Downey
Music Pub.
BMI

1001-2
VOCAL & INST.
2:24

THUMP DE DE DUM DUM
(J. Maniscalco)
ERNIE BAPTISTE

Jack Bee

Downey Music
Pub. Co.
BMI

WR-1004
Time 2:03
K8OW-5005

VOO DOO DOLLY
(Jimmie Hombs-Eddie Richards)
JIMMIE HOMBS
with THE INVICTAS and
THE HOLLYWOOD
REBELS
13117 LAKEWOOD BLVD. DOWNEY, CALIFORNIA

FLAIR **FLIP**

FRATERNITY

GOLDEN STATE **GOLDWAX**

GWP

METEOR

MIRWOOD

ACE RECORDS

SPECIALTY

ACKNOWLEDGEMENTS

ACKNOWLEDGEMENTS

From the writer:
My thanks to Neil Scaplehorn, Trevor Churchill, Roger Armstrong, Ted Carroll, Vicki Fox, Carol Fawcett, Ady Croadsell, Peter Gibbon, Tony Rounce, Dean Rudland, Nick Garrard, Alec Palao, Rob Finnis, Philip Chevron, Charlie Gillett, Carol Clerk and Eve (for photocopying).

From Ace Records:
They also served—Ace employees and consultants past and present*.

Not everyone has a great story about discovering rare master-tapes, but a record company doesn't run without accounts departments, salesmen, warehouse staff, press officers—the list is endless. Everyone mentioned below has played as important a part in the Ace story.

Sheila and Maureen
Anne Pitts
Khayer Ott-Mia
Vermillion Sands
Donna Cotten (Feldman)
Gisela Roberts
Yvette DeRoy*
Chris Popham
Chris Morrison
Chris O'Donnell
John Logan
Helen Thornton
Mike Beard
Paul Bracegirdle
Tracie Hill
Des Parks
Russ Dewbury
John Broven
Richard Bowser
George Seuref
John Crosby
Cheryl Rego
Rob Hughes
Yvonne Sookha
John Fry
Steve Morgan
Dave Cunningham
Jessica Rant
Bob Dunham*

Chris Harper
Brigitte Barthes
Nicky McCarthy (Kenyon)
Dominique Holmes
Julia Honeywell
Andrew Buckley
Christine Thornton
Chris Lines*
Andy Menikou*
Neil Scaplehorn*
Liz Buckley*
Leroy Kew*
Deji Odekeye
Carl Ferguson*
Karen Spearing
Jorge Cortes*
Damon Vallero*
Mick Patrick*
Marty Wekser
Graham Sharpe*

Sound Mastering:
Adam Skeaping*
Duncan Cowell*
Nick Robbins*
Rob Shread*
Dave Young
Bob Jones

© 2007 Black Dog Publishing Limited, London, UK,
the artists and authors. All rights reserved.

Commissioned by Nadine Käthe Monem at Black Dog Publishing.
Edited by Blanche Craig at Black Dog Publishing.
Designed by Matthew Pull at Black Dog Publishing.

Black Dog Publishing Limited
10A Acton Street
London WC1X 9NG
United Kingdom

info@blackdogonline.com
www.blackdogonline.com

British Library Cataloguing-in-Publication Data.

A CIP record for this book is available from the British Library.

ISBN: 978 1 906155 03 2

Black Dog Publishing Limited, London, UK, is an
environmentally responsible company. *Ace Records* is
printed on NopaSet, high white woodfree uncoated
matt paper, chlorine free, FSC certified.